Windows Shortcut Keys

In File Manager

KEY SEQUENCE	EFFECT
Directory tree only:	
+	Expand one level
*	Expand branch
Ctrl-*	Expand all
–	Collapse branch
Directory window only:	
Shift-↑ *or* Shift-↓	Extended selection
Ctrl-/	Select all

In Print Manager

KEY SEQUENCE	EFFECT
Alt-P	Pause processing print queue
Alt-R	Resume processing print queue
Alt-D	Delete print job

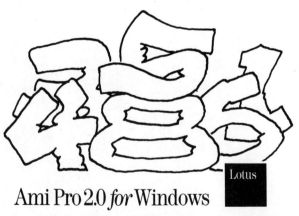

How to get **oohs**, *ahs*, and **WOWS** from your facts, figures, and forecasts.

Introducing Lotus® Freelance Graphics™ for Windows.™ It's the fastest, easiest, and most enjoyable way to create show-stopping slides, overheads, and handouts. Instantly.

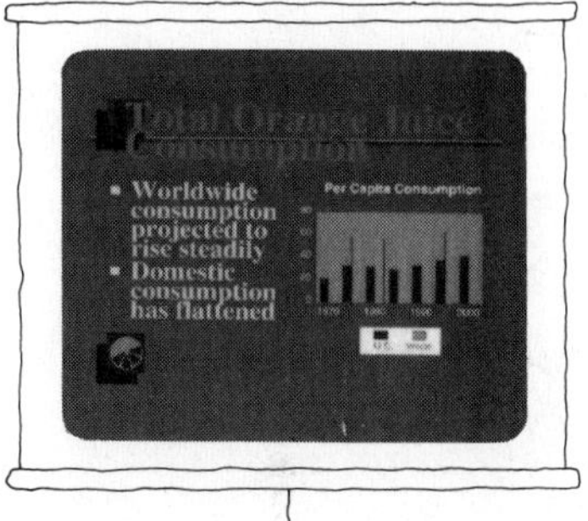

What's more, Freelance Graphics features SmartIcons™ like those in Lotus 1-2-3® for Windows. Plus, it has the tightest integration with the Lotus suite of Windows applications–giving you direct access to your spreadsheets, word processing documents, and existing graphics.

Get a sneak preview now by ordering a Freelance Graphics demo disk. It's yours for the asking. And it's free!

For your free demo disk, call:

1-800-872-3387, ext. 6223.

Freelance Graphics *for* Windows

Lotus

Windows™ 3.0 Instant Reference

Marshall L. Moseley

San Francisco • Paris • Düsseldorf • Soest

Acquisitions Editor: Dianne King
Series Editor: James A. Compton
Editor: Savitha Pichai
Technical Editor: Michael Gross
Word Processors: Lisa Mitchell, Ann Dunn, Scott Campbell, Paul Erickson
Series Designer: Ingrid Owen
Pasteup Artist: Lisa Jaffe
Screen Graphics: Cuong Le
Desktop Publishing Specialists: M.D. Barrera, Dan Brodnitz
Proofreaders: Edith Rex, Lisa Haden
Indexer: Nancy Anderman Guenther
Cover Designer: Archer Design

Library of Congress Card Number: 90-71671
ISBN: 0-89588-757-6

Manufactured in the United States of America

10 9 8 7

SYBEX INSTANT REFERENCES

We've designed SYBEX *Instant References* to meet the evolving needs of software users, who want essential information easily accessible, in a clear and concise form. Our best authors have distilled their expertise into compact reference guides in which you can look up the precise steps for using any feature, including the available options. More than just summaries, these books also provide insights into effective usage drawn from our authors' wealth of experience.

Other SYBEX Instant References are:

dBASE IV 1.1 Programmer's Instant Reference
Alan Simpson

AutoCAD Instant Reference
George Omura

dBASE IV 1.1 User's Instant Reference
Alan Simpson

DOS Instant Reference
Greg Harvey and Kay Yarborough Nelson

Harvard Graphics Instant Reference
Gerald Jones

Lotus 1-2-3 Instant Reference, Release 2.2
Greg Harvey and Kay Yarborough Nelson

Norton Utilities 5 Instant Reference
Michael Gross

PC Tools Deluxe 6 Instant Reference
Gordon McComb

WordPerfect 5 Instant Reference
Greg Harvey and Kay Yarborough Nelson

WordPerfect 5.1 Instant Reference
Greg Harvey and Kay Yarborough Nelson

For Dean Irwin, Doug Caffarel, and Mark Slonim, good friends through the good times. Thanks guys.

Acknowledgments

The author would like to thank his wife, Pam Dillehay, for her love and unwavering support during this project.

Table of Contents

Chapter 1

THE PROGRAM MANAGER

Chapter 2

Switching between Windows

Chapter 3

Windows Help

Chapter 4

The Clipboard

Chapter 5

The File Manager

Chapter 6

Setting Up and Configuring Windows

Chapter 7

The Print Manager

Chapter 8

The Macro Recorder

Chapter 9

The PIF Editor

Chapter 10

Windows Text Editing

Chapter 11

Paintbrush

Chapter 12

Communications with Windows Terminal

Chapter 13

Miscellaneous Accessory Programs

Introduction

The idea behind this book is simple. When you are stymied by a command in Windows 3.0 that does not work as you intended, or when you want a quick refresher about a certain procedure, you need a single source of information that can quickly help you solve the problem at hand and get on with your work.

This book is intended to do just that. It will quickly give you the information necessary to get the most from Windows 3.0's multitude of features. It will supply instructions on Windows' basic commands and its most sophisticated functions. Windows 3.0 is substantially different from previous versions of Windows and this book is intended for use only with this version.

Because we expect you to consult this book as a reference for solving day-to-day problems, we have assumed that your copy of the program is already installed. In addition, because Windows can be customized in many ways to suit individual preferences, we have not attempted to describe customization in detail here. For detailed information on installation, customization features, and advanced topics, see *Mastering Windows 3.0*, also from SYBEX.

HOW THIS BOOK IS ORGANIZED

This book is divided into 13 chapters. Chapters 1–7 describe the procedures you need to know to run, move, and size Windows programs. They also describe the utility programs that are a necessary part of using Windows on a day-to-day basis.

Chapters 8–13 describe the accessory applications, or "mini-apps" as Microsoft calls them, that are included with Windows 3.0. These include programs for recording and executing macros, painting and drawing, telecommunications, scheduling appointments, and creating documents.

Each reference entry contains a concise series of instructions that address a specific procedure or function. Each entry generally contains the following sections:

- Explanation—this section succinctly describes the subject matter of the entry. In "Minimizing a Window," for example, this section explains what minimizing a window means and how it fits into the overall Windows structure.
- To Use the Mouse/Keyboard—this section lists the series of mouse actions or keystrokes you must execute to perform the procedure under discussion. We have chosen to give precedence to mouse commands rather than keyboard commands because Windows is most efficiently used with a mouse.

Where appropriate, entries also include:

- Notes—this section contains information that you should know to fully understand the reference entry. This information can take many forms: for example, warnings of how the procedure under discussion could affect other executing programs, or a description of how the procedure could enhance or degrade Windows' performance.
- See Also—this section contains cross-references to headings in this book that are related to the current procedure.

OVERVIEW OF WINDOWS 3.0

Windows 3.0 is a program that provides a graphic user interface (GUI) for IBM and IBM-compatible personal computers. When running Windows 3.0, the computer user interacts with the computer visually. Rather than type commands, the user moves a small arrow, called a pointer, around on screen and selects commands. Programs appear on screen in rectangular areas called windows. Each window can be sized and moved around on screen. Multiple programs can appear on screen at the same time, and they can operate simultaneously.

Windows 3.0 runs two types of programs: standard DOS applications and Windows-specific applications. A standard DOS application is any DOS program that is not written specifically for the Windows environment. Using Windows 3.0, you can run such popular programs as WordPerfect and Lotus 1-2-3. Standard DOS applications can use the full display screen, or run in a window. A Windows-specific application is one written explicitly for the Windows environment. Once run, it appears as a window. It can be sized and moved around on screen. It can also be placed in the background, or allowed to take up the entire screen.

Windows 3.0 displays programs, files, and disks as icons, much like the Macintosh from Apple Computer, Inc. (An icon is a picture that represents a resource within the computing system. A memo might be represented on screen by a picture of a piece of paper, while a printer might be represented by a picture of a printer.)

When Windows 3.0 first runs, you are presented with a primary window called the Program Manager. The Program Manager contains a set of icons called *program groups*. One of these groups, the Main group, is opened to a window, revealing still more icons. These are *program items*. These items represent the programs you can run from within Windows 3.0

Windows 3.0 takes advantage of the 80386 and 80286 microprocessors used in today's most powerful microcomputers. It uses the protected mode of those systems. In protected mode, memory is reserved for each program and no other programs may use that memory—it is protected. Windows also accesses up to 16 Mb of memory.

Windows 3.0 is "network aware." This means that if a personal computer running Windows 3.0 is connected to a local area network (LAN), Windows will see the connection and provide access to the network and to network resources.

Windows 3.0 is a boon for users of MS-DOS personal computers. They no longer need to understand the complex syntax of MS-DOS commands. Windows 3.0 provides a standard, usable, powerful interface for all programs under MS-DOS.

TYPOGRAPHICAL AND INSTRUCTIONAL CONVENTIONS

Each entry in this book is designed to provide you with a clear, concise explanation of a particular Windows 3.0 procedure or function. To that end, information is presented here in a particular manner.

Words or terms that require special emphasis are italicized. Emphasized words can be special Windows 3.0 terms, such as *scroll bar* or *control panel*. Words and terms are usually emphasized only once, when they are defined, and are printed normally thereafter.

Command names, menu items, and dialog box names are printed with initial capital letters. Some examples are: the Program Manager, the File menu, and the Save As command.

Text that represents a matter unique to your specific situation is indicated by italics. For example, if you need to key in a drive letter, the instructions will ask for your *Drive*. You will substitute the actual drive letter for the word in italics.

The names of keys are printed exactly as they appear on a standard IBM keyboard—for example, PgDn and NumLock. Directory names and file names are printed in all capital letters.

When an instruction directs you to perform a mouse action and then "click left," you should then click on the left mouse button.

Chapter 1

THE PROGRAM MANAGER

The Program Manager is the Windows utility that runs applications. It starts automatically when you run Windows, and exiting (or *closing*) it is the only way to leave Windows.

Before you can use the Program Manager effectively, you must first understand the types of windows and icons that Windows uses. There are two types of windows, as explained below:

- Application windows—these contain executing Windows programs. They can be sized and moved anywhere on the Windows desktop.
- Document windows—these are generated by an application window. A document window cannot be sized or moved outside the confines of its parent application window. Document windows are manipulated in the same way as ordinary windows, except they use slightly different key commands.

Additionally, there are three types of icons:

- Application icons—these are minimized application windows. A minimized program is one that is still running, but has been reduced to an icon that appears at the bottom of the Windows desktop.
- Document icons—these are minimized document windows. They appear within an application window's workspace.
- Program item icons—these are icons that appear only within the Program Manager. They will start applications and, optionally, load their associated documents.

When you run Windows for the first time, the Program Manager appears on screen, as shown in Figure 1.1. Within the primary Program Manager window, there are secondary windows called *group windows.* They appear on screen as fully opened windows, such as the one titled Main in Figure 1.1, or as group icons, which are located below the Main window in the same figure. Group windows are document windows, and group icons are document icons.

Within each group window are program item icons that represent individual application programs. By selecting a program item icon, you can run the program that it represents. Program item icons can be moved between program groups, copied, or renamed. They can also be configured to execute in unique ways that suit your individual needs. For example, a program item icon might automatically run your word processor and open a specific memorandum or report.

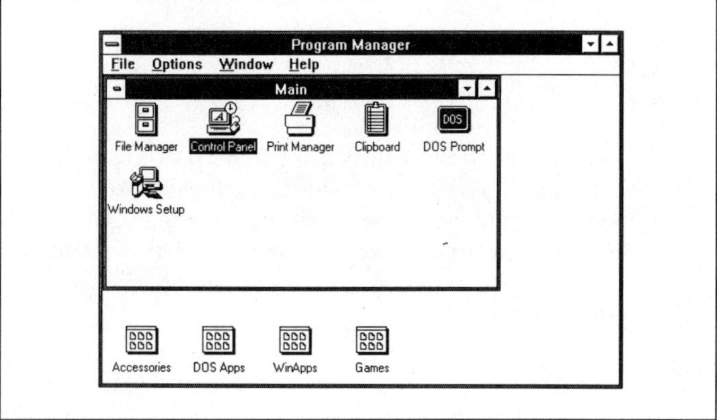

Figure 1.1: The Program manager

OPENING A WINDOW

• EXPLANATION To open a window is to make some portion of Windows—a program or a component of a program—active. In the Program Manager, when you open a document icon, a document window opens. When you open a program item icon, the program runs.

There are two ways to open a window in Windows 3.0: by selecting an icon from within the Program Manager and opening it, as outlined below, or by using the File Manager to select a file and run it or the program associated with it (see Chapter 5, "Running a Program from File Manager").

To run a program, you should first open its group window.

To Use the Mouse

- Double-click the mouse pointer on the icon of the window you wish to open. When you double-click on an icon, it will run right away. If you have selected a group icon, a Group Window will open. If you have selected a program icon, the program will run.

An alternative method is to use the Program Manager's menu system to open a Window.

1. Select the icon of the window you wish to open by placing the mouse pointer on it and clicking once.
2. Pull down the File menu by clicking on the word *File* in the menu bar.
3. Select Open. The program associated with the icon you selected will run.

To Use the Keyboard

- Using the direction keys, highlight the icon of the window you wish to open (the program you wish to run), and press ↵.

See Also Opening a Directory Window (Ch. 5), Maximizing a Group Window, Switching between Groups (Ch. 1)

MINIMIZING A WINDOW

• EXPLANATION To *minimize* a window is to make it disappear from the Windows desktop and reappear at the bottom of the screen as an icon. The program continues to run and remains in exactly the state it was in when you minimized it. You minimize a window by clicking on the minimize button—which is an arrow pointing downward in the upper-right corner of the window (see Figure 1.2)—or by using the menu system to select the Minimize option.

To Use the Mouse

- Place the mouse pointer on the Minimize button and click left. The window will disappear and its icon will appear at the bottom of the desktop, unless the window is a document window, in which case the icon appears at the bottom of the application window's workspace.

An alternative method is to use the menu system to select the Minimize option.

1. Pull down the Control menu of the program you wish to minimize by clicking on the Control menu symbol in the upper-left corner of the window.
2. Select Minimize.

To Use the Keyboard

1. With the window you wish to minimize active, press Alt-Spacebar. The Control menu in the upper-left corner of the window will drop down.
2. Type **N**.

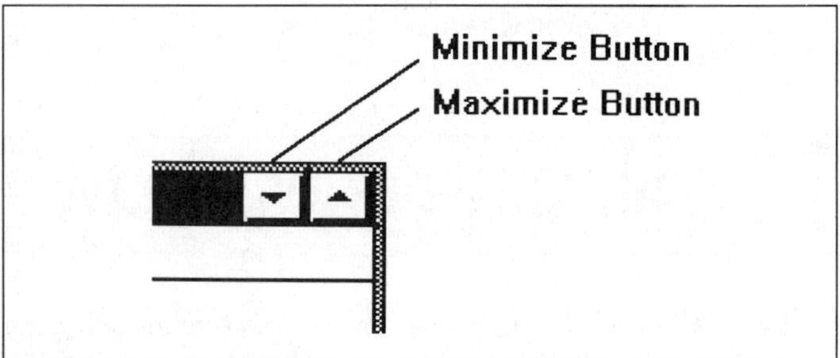

Figure 1.2: The Minimize and Maximize buttons

See Also Opening a Window, Maximizing a Window

MAXIMIZING A WINDOW

• EXPLANATION To *maximize* a window is to cause either an icon or a window to expand and take up the entire screen. A maximized window has no borders, so you can't manipulate its size; and it has a new symbol called the Restore button, consisting of a double-headed arrow, in the upper-right corner of the window.

A window is maximized when you click on the Maximize button—which is an arrow pointing upward in the upper-right corner of the window (see Figure 1.2)—or when you use the menu system to select the Maximize option.

To Use the Mouse

- Place the mouse pointer on the Maximize button in the upper-right corner of the window and click left. The program will expand to take up the entire desktop.

An alternative method is to use the menu system to select the Maximize option.

1. Pull down the Control menu of the program you wish to maximize by clicking on the Control menu symbol in the upper-left corner of the window.
2. Select Maximize.

To Use the Keyboard

1. With the window you wish to maximize active, press Alt-Spacebar. The Control menu in the upper-left corner of the window will drop down.
2. Type **X**.

See Also Minimizing a Window, Opening a Window

RESTORING A WINDOW

• EXPLANATION To *restore* a window is to cause either a program icon or a maximized window to return to its original place and size on the desktop.

When restoring a maximized window, you click on the Restore button, which is a dual-headed arrow in the upper right portion of the screen (see Figure 1.3), or use the menu system to select the Restore option. When restoring an icon, you double-click on it, or use the key combination Alt-Tab to select and restore it.

See Also Restoring a Group Window, Restoring a Maximized Group Window

To Restore a Maximized Window

Mouse

- Place the mouse pointer on the Restore button and click left. The program will to return to its original state on the desktop.

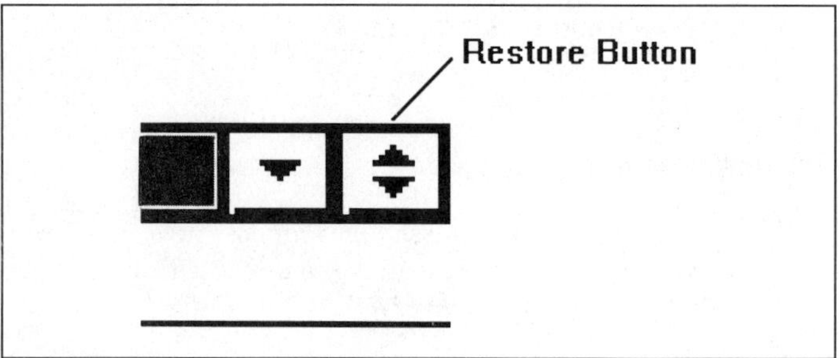

Figure 1.3: The Restore button

An alternative method is to use the menu system to select the Restore option.

1. Pull down the Control menu of the program you wish to Restore by clicking on the Control menu symbol in the upper-left corner of the window.
2. Select Restore.

Keyboard

1. With the maximized window on screen, press Alt-Spacebar. The Control menu in the upper-left corner of the window will drop down. If you are restoring a maximized document window, press Alt-Hyphen instead of Alt-Spacebar.
2. Type **R**.

To Restore an Icon

Mouse

- Place the mouse pointer on the icon you wish to restore and double-click. The program will to return to its original state on the desktop.

Keyboard

1. To select the icon you wish to restore, press Alt-Esc. You may have multiple icons on the desktop, so if necessary, continue to hold the Alt key down and repeatedly press the Esc key. If you are in the Program Manager window and moving between document icons, use the arrow keys, not Alt-Esc. When the icon you wish to restore becomes highlighted, release the Alt-Esc keys.
2. Press Alt-Spacebar. The icon's Control menu will appear. If you are working with a document window, press Alt-Hyphen.
3. Type **R**. The icon will disappear and the program will return to its original state on the desktop.

CLOSING A WINDOW

• EXPLANATION To *close* a window is to render it inactive, at which time it disappears from the desktop. If you close the Program Manager, Windows will stop running and the DOS prompt will return.

If the window being closed is an application program, the program ceases running. If it is a document window, the program that generated it remains active.

There are two ways to close a window in Windows 3.0—by using the mouse or the keyboard.

To Use the Mouse

1. Place the mouse pointer on the Control menu of the program you wish to close and click left.
2. Click on Close.

The window should close. If you have been doing work of some kind in the window, and haven't saved it recently, you may see a dialog box asking you to save or abandon the work. Reply to the query and the window will close.

To Use the Keyboard

- With the window you wish to close active, press Alt-F4. If you are closing a Document window, press Ctrl-F4.

MOVING A WINDOW

• EXPLANATION It is possible to move and place windows anywhere on the desktop. Document windows may only be moved within the window that generated them, while standard windows can be moved anywhere. When a window is moved over another window, it covers that window. It is possible for windows to cover each other completely.

Moving a window is accomplished in two ways: by clicking and dragging on the window's title bar (see Figure 1.4), or by using the keyboard's direction keys.

To Use the Mouse

1. Place the mouse pointer on the title bar of the window you wish to move. Click on the left mouse button and hold it down. This will "attach" the window to the pointer, so they can be moved around on screen as a single unit.
2. Move the window to its desired position, and release the mouse button.

To Use the Keyboard

1. With the window you wish to move on screen and active, press Alt-Spacebar. The Control menu will drop down. If you are in a document window, press Alt-Hyphen.
2. Type **M**.
3. Press and hold one of the arrow keys and move the window to its desired position. Note that you can only move

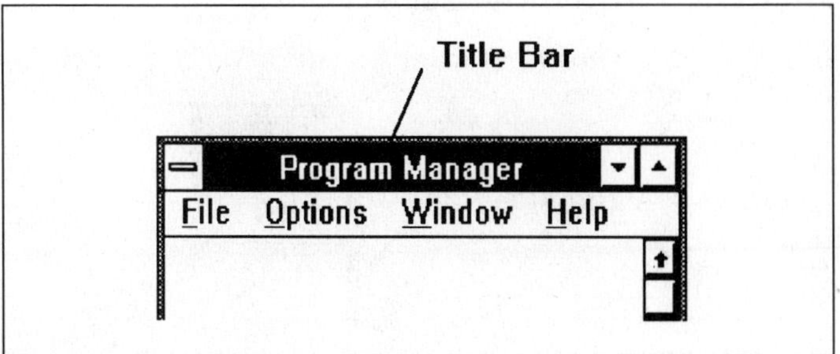

Figure 1.4: The title bar

vertically or horizontally with arrow keys. If you need to move diagonally, use a mouse.

4. Press ↵.

SIZING A WINDOW

• EXPLANATION The size of a window can easily be changed. The width and the height can be changed independently or at the same time. Document windows may only be sized within the window that generated them, while standard windows can be adjusted to any size.

There are two ways to size a window: by clicking and dragging the window's borders, or by using the keyboard's direction keys.

There are three types of window borders: horizontal, vertical, and corner (see Figure 1.5). As you move the mouse pointer over these borders, its appearance changes. When positioned over the horizontal border, the pointer becomes a vertical line with arrowheads at each end. The new pointer indicates the directions in which you can move the border—in this case, up or down. When positioned over a vertical border, it becomes a horizontal line with arrowheads at

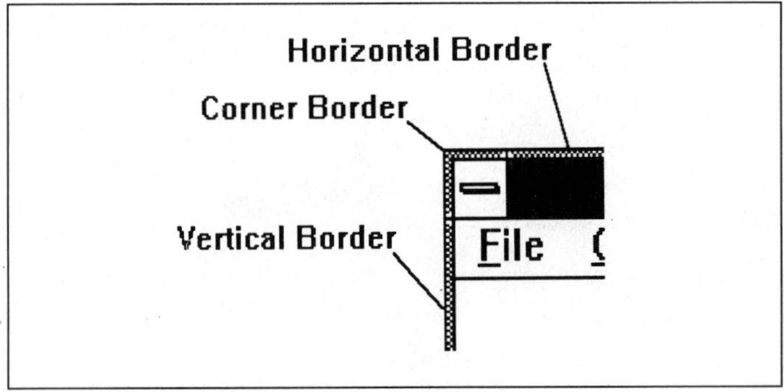

Figure 1.5: Three types of window borders

each end, indicating that you can move the border left or right. Over a corner border, it becomes a diagonal line with arrowheads at each end, showing that the height and width of the window can be adjusted simultaneously.

To Use the Mouse

1. Place the mouse pointer on the border of the window you wish to size; click on the left mouse button and hold it down. This will "grab" the window border, so it can now be moved.
2. Move the border to its desired position, and release the mouse button.

If you grabbed a horizontal or vertical border, you can only change the height or width. To change both at the same time, you need to grab a corner border.

See Also Tiling and Cascading Application Windows (Ch. 2), Arranging Multiple Group Windows—Tile and Cascade

MOVING AN ICON

• **EXPLANATION** It is possible to move icons from one location on the desktop to another. Document icons, which appear only in the document windows, may only be moved around within their parent application windows.

To Use the Mouse

1. Place the mouse pointer on the icon you wish to move. Click on the left mouse button and hold it down.
2. Move the icon to its desired position, and release the mouse button.

GROUP WINDOWS

• EXPLANATION Within the Program Manager window, there are secondary windows called *group windows*. They appear on screen as fully opened document windows or as document icons (see Figure 1.6). Group windows are document windows, and they carry with them the limitations of document windows. Note that document icons cannot be moved outside the Program Manager window, and they always appear as shaded rectangles with smaller rectangles inside them.

Group windows organize programs into discrete, related sets. One Group window, for example, may contain all programs associated with word processing, while another may be for telecommunications. Windows comes with three default group windows: Main, Accessories, and Games. You may also have chosen to install Windows application and/or non-Windows application group windows.

When a group window is open, the icons for the programs you can run are contained within. You can maximize or minimize group

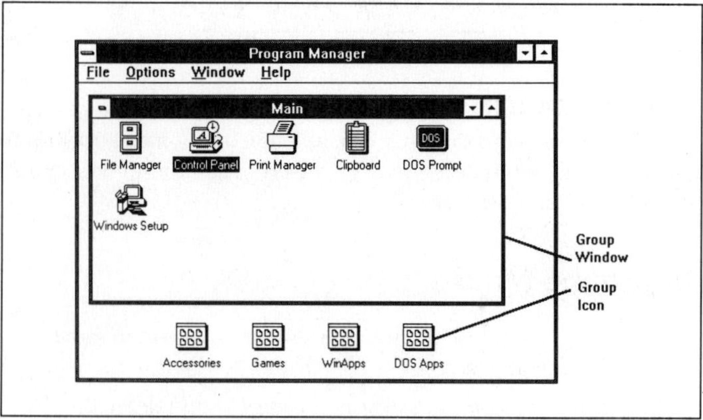

Figure 1.6: The Program Manager window

windows, add programs to them, delete programs from them, and move or copy programs between them.

RESTORING A GROUP WINDOW

● **EXPLANATION** When the Program Manager is first open, only one group window is opened. All the others are displayed in the form of document icons (see Figure 1.6). By restoring a document icon, you can change it into an open group window.

To Use the Mouse

- Double-click on the document icon you wish to restore.

The document icon's menu system supplies a less direct, but better documented, method.

1. Place the mouse pointer over the document icon you wish to restore and click left once. The icon's Control menu will appear.
2. Select Restore.

To Use the Keyboard

Start by making sure the Program Manager window is open, and that the document icons you are working with are visible within it.

1. Press Ctrl-Tab repeatedly to select each document icon in turn. Release the Ctrl-Tab keys when the icon you wish to restore is selected.
2. Press ↵.

MINIMIZING A GROUP WINDOW

● **EXPLANATION** To minimize a group window is to cause it to disappear from inside the Program Manager window, and reappear at the bottom of the window as a document icon.

To Use the Mouse

1. Place the mouse pointer on the Minimize button in the upper-right corner of the group window.
2. Click on the left mouse button; the group window will disappear and its document icon will appear at the bottom of the Program Manager window.

An alternative method is to use the menu system to select the Minimize option.

1. Pull down the Control menu of the group window you wish to minimize by clicking on the Control menu symbol.
2. Select Minimize.

To Use the Keyboard

1. With the window you wish to minimize active, press Alt-Hyphen. The Control menu will drop down.
2. Type **N**.

MAXIMIZING A GROUP WINDOW

• **EXPLANATION** To maximize a group window is to make it expand within the Program Manager window so that it takes up the entire window.

To Use the Mouse

- Place the mouse pointer on the Maximize button in the upper-right corner of the group window, and click left. The group window will expand to take up the entire Program Manager window.

An alternative method is to use the menu system to select the Maximize option.

1. Pull down the Control menu of the group window you wish to minimize by clicking on the Control menu symbol in the upper-left corner of the window.

2. Select Maximize.

To Use the Keyboard

1. With the window you wish to maximize active, press Alt-Hyphen. The Control menu in the upper-left corner of the window will drop down.
2. Type **M**.

RESTORING A MAXIMIZED GROUP

• EXPLANATION When a group window is maximized, the upper-right corner of the Program Manager window changes to a three-button configuration: a Minimize button, a Maximize button, and a Restore button (see Figure 1.7). The Minimize and Maximize buttons act upon the Program Manager window as a whole, and do not affect group windows. The Restore button, however, changes the maximized group window back into an open document window. If you maximized the current group window when it was a document icon, the Restore button will not turn it back into an icon; it will make it an open window.

To Use the Mouse

- Place the mouse pointer on the Restore button in the upper-right corner of the group window, and click the left mouse button. The maximized group window will shrink and become a standard group window.

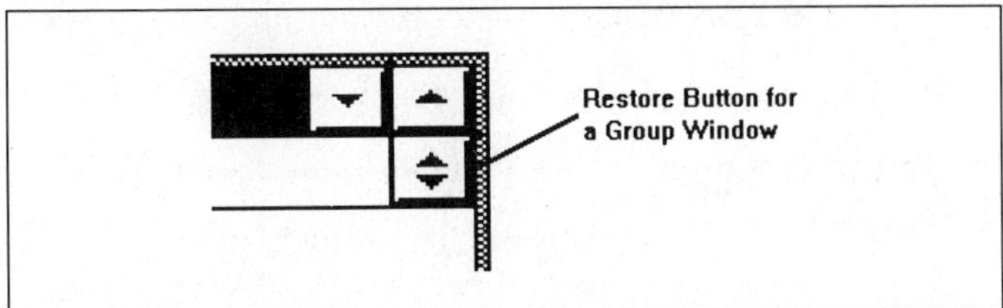

Figure 1.7: The Restore button on a maximized group window

An alternative method is to use the menu system to select the Restore option.

1. Pull down the Control menu of the group window you wish to restore by clicking on the Control menu symbol in the upper-left corner of the window.
2. Select Restore.

To Use the Keyboard

1. With the window you wish to restore active, press Alt-Hyphen. The Control menu in the upper-left corner of the window will drop down.
2. Type **R**.

SWITCHING BETWEEN GROUPS

• **EXPLANATION** When there are multiple groups on screen, whether they are group windows or group icons, you may want to switch from one group to another. When you switch groups, the currently active group becomes inactive, and the new group—the one you have switched to—becomes active. You can distinguish the currently active group window by its colored title bar and border.

To Use the Mouse

- Place the mouse pointer over the group window or document icon you wish to switch to, and click left.

To Use the Keyboard

1. Press Ctrl-Tab. This will make each group window and group icon active in succession.
2. When the group window or group icon you wish to switch to is selected, release the Ctrl and Tab keys.

ADDING A PROGRAM TO A GROUP

• EXPLANATION There are many reasons to add a program to a group window. You may have purchased new software, and now wish to make it accessible from Windows, or you may have old software that you wish to invoke from Windows.

There are two ways to add a program to a group window: Use the File Manager to display a list of files, and "drag" the desired program file into the group window; or use the Program Manager's menu system to key in the name of the program you want to add to the group. The first method is explained under "Creating a Program Icon" in Chapter 5.

To Use the Program Manager Menus

1. Open the group window to which you wish to add a program.
2. Pull down the Program Manager's File menu.
3. Select New. A dialog box will appear with two option buttons in it: New Program Group and New Program Item.
4. Select New Program Item and click on OK. A dialog box will appear with two entry fields in it, one for a description of the program and another for the path and file specification of the program itself.
5. Type a description of the program in the description field and press Tab.
6. Type the path and file specification of the program you wish to add, then press ↵. If you are not sure of the path name or file specification, click on the Browse button. A list of files in the current directory will appear. You can move to the parent directory of the current directory by clicking on the two dots (..) at the top of the list. You can also select different drives by clicking on the appropriate drive letter.
7. When you find the file you want, double-click on it.

DELETING A PROGRAM ITEM FROM A GROUP

• **EXPLANATION** When you delete a program file from your hard disk, you should also delete the program item that invoked it. It is also worthwhile to keep in mind that when you delete a program item, you do not delete the file on disk that the program item invokes.

To Use the Mouse

1. Open the group window that contains the program you wish to delete.
2. Select the program by clicking once on its icon.
3. Pull down the File menu and select Delete. You will see a dialog box that asks you to confirm the program's deletion.
4. Select Yes.

To Use the Keyboard

1. Open the group window that contains the program you wish to delete.
2. Press either ← or → repeatedly until the icon of the program you wish to delete is highlighted.
3. Press Del. You will see a dialog box that asks you to confirm the program's deletion.
4. Select Yes by pressing ↵.

COPYING A PROGRAM BETWEEN GROUPS

• **EXPLANATION** There are two ways to copy a program item between groups: Use the mouse to "drag" a program item from one group to another, thus copying it; or use the Copy option that is available in the Windows menu system.

To Use the Mouse

1. Open the group window containing the program you wish to copy.
2. Open the group window that you wish to contain the copy.
3. Press and hold the Ctrl key.

4. Place the mouse pointer on the program icon you wish to copy, then "grab" the icon by clicking on the left mouse button and holding it down.
5. Move the icon to the destination group window.
6. Release the mouse button and the Ctrl key.

To Use the Menus

1. Open the group window containing the program you wish to copy.
2. Select the Program Item you wish to copy, by pressing ← or → until the item is highlighted.
3. Pull down the Program Manager's File menu by pressing Alt-F.
4. Type C. You will see a dialog box with a drop-down box inside it. In the drop-down box will be the name of the group window that is first in alphabetical sequence (usually Accessories).
5. To see a list of all the available group windows, press Alt-↓.
6. Use ↑ and ↓ to move through the list of group windows, until the one that you want to hold the copy is highlighted.
7. Press ↵.

MOVING A PROGRAM BETWEEN GROUPS

• **EXPLANATION** There are two ways to move a program item between groups: Use the mouse to "drag" a program item from one group to another; or use the Move option that is available in the Windows menu system.

To Use the Mouse

1. Open the group window containing the program you wish to copy.
2. Open the group window that you wish to contain the copy.

3. Place the mouse pointer on the program icon you wish to copy, then "grab" the icon by clicking on the mouse button and holding it down.
4. Move the icon to the destination group window.
5. Release the mouse button.

To Use the Menus

1. Open the group window containing the program you wish to copy.
2. Select the program item you wish to copy, by pressing ← or → until the item is highlighted.
3. Pull down the Program Manager's File menu by pressing Alt-F.
4. Type **M**. You will see a dialog box with a drop-down box inside it. In the drop-down box will be the name of the currently selected group window.
5. To see a list of all the available group windows, press Alt-↓.
6. Use ↑ and ↓ to move through the list of group windows, until the one that you want is highlighted.
7. Press ↵.

ARRANGING MULTIPLE GROUP WINDOWS—TILE AND CASCADE

• EXPLANATION If you open more than two group windows at a time, the Program Manager window can get crowded. It becomes difficult to see which windows are open and what program items they contain. To solve this problem, the Program Manager has two commands—Cascade and Tile—that automatically size and place group windows.

When open group windows are displayed in a cascade, they overlap each other, with only one window visible—the one that was active when Cascade was selected (see Figure 1.8). When open group windows are tiled, the space provided by the Program Manager is evenly divided among the group windows. The groups are arranged on screen so they don't overlap. At least some portion of the desktop area of each group is visible (see Figure 1.9).

Before selecting either Cascade or Tile, make sure the group windows that you want to arrange are open.

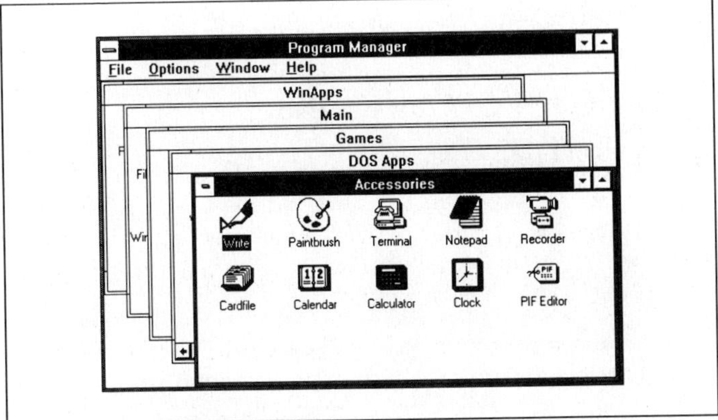

Figure 1.8: Program groups in a cascade

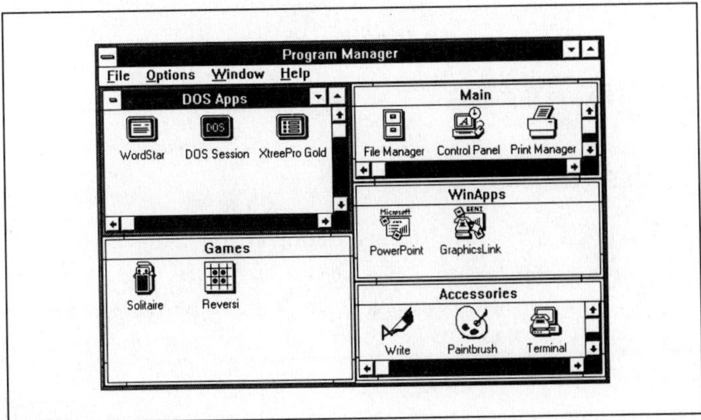

Figure 1.9: Tiled program groups

To Cascade or Tile Group Windows

Mouse

1. Pull down the Window menu of the Program Manager.
2. Select Cascade or Tile.

Keyboard

- Press Shift-F5 (Cascade) or Shift-F4 (Tile).

ARRANGING GROUP ICONS

• EXPLANATION Windows will arrange all the icons within the Program Manager into neat rows and columns. If a group window is active, it will arrange the program item icons within that window. If no group window is active, it will arrange the group icons in the Program Manager workspace.

Whether you are using a mouse or a keyboard, open the group window containing the icons you wish to arrange. If you wish to arrange group icons, make sure all group windows are closed.

To Use the Mouse

1. Select the Window menu in the Program Manager.
2. Select Arrange Icons. All group icons will appear in a neat row at the bottom of the Program Manager window.

To Use the Keyboard

1. Press Alt-W to select the Window menu in the Program Manager.
2. Type **A** to select Arrange Icons. All group icons will appear in a neat row at the bottom of the Program Manager window.

See Also Arranging Application Icons (Ch. 2)

ADDING A GROUP WINDOW

• **EXPLANATION** There are many reasons to add (create) a new group window. You may have installed a new type of software on your hard disk and now need a group window to keep it organized. Or you may want to organize your old programs in a new way—for example, by placing all your word processing programs in a single group window.

To Use the Mouse

1. Pull down the Program Manager File menu, and select New. A dialog box will appear with two option buttons in it, one labeled Program Group, the other labeled Program Item.
2. If it is not selected already, select Program Group and click on OK. A dialog box will appear with two entry fields. The first one is for a description of the group window. That description will appear in the title bar of the group window and below the group icon. The other field is for the name of the file that will hold the group information. If you leave this blank, the Program Manager will automatically generate a file name with a .GRP extension. You can, however, specify a name, following the DOS file name format. It is probably wise to give the file a name that is similar to the group name (i.e., if the group is called "Word Processing," use the file name "WORDPROC.GRP").
3. Type a description of the group window, then press Tab.
4. If you wish, type a file name for the group.
5. Select OK.

To Use the Keyboard

1. Press Alt-F to pull down the Program Manager File menu.
2. Type **N** for New. A dialog box will appear with two option buttons in it, one labeled Program Group, the other labeled Program Item.

3. Use ↑ or ↓ to select Program Group, if it is not selected already, then press ↵. A dialog box will appear with two entry fields. The first one is for a description of the group window. That description will appear in the title bar of the group window and below the group icon. The other field is for the name of the file that will hold the group information. If you leave this blank, the Program Manager will automatically generate a file with a .GRP extension. You can, however, specify a name, following the DOS file name format. It is probably wise to give the file a name that is similar to the group name (i.e., if the group is called "Word Processing," use the file name "WORDPROC.GRP").
4. Type a description of the group window, then press Tab.
5. If you wish, type a file name for the group.
6. Press ↵.

DELETING A GROUP WINDOW

• EXPLANATION When you eliminate a program or a group of programs from your hard disk, you should delete the group window that housed them. Deleting a group window also deletes all the program item icons within that group, and you will *not* be prompted before they are deleted.

To delete a group window, it should be closed and in the form of a group icon. If you attempt to delete an open group window, Windows will assume you want to delete the currently selected program item within it.

To Use the Mouse

1. Select the group icon of the group window you wish to delete.
2. Pull down the File menu and select Delete. You will see a dialog box asking you if you really wish to delete the selected group window.
3. Select Yes.

To Use the Keyboard

1. Select the group icon of the group window you wish to delete, using the arrow keys to move between group icons until the one you want is highlighted.
2. Press Del. You will see a dialog box asking you if you really wish to delete the selected group window.
3. Select Yes by pressing ↵.

Chapter 2

SWITCHING BETWEEN WINDOWS

As you use Windows, you may want to switch between multiple windows, or between windows and icons. Windows 3.0 provides two facilities for doing this: key commands, which allow you to move quickly from window to window, and a utility program called Task List that allows you to move between windows by choosing from a list of active programs. Task List also allows you to shut down applications or arrange their appearance on the desktop.

THE KEY COMMANDS

Windows provides two key commands that allow you to switch quickly between windows: Alt-Esc and Alt-Tab. Unlike Alt-Esc, Alt-Tab also makes the selected window active.

ALT-ESC

Alt-Esc will make the currently active window inactive, and move to the next window in sequence. The sequence is determined by the order in which the programs were first invoked.

When you switch to an application icon using Alt-Esc, the icon becomes selected, but nothing else happens. To restore or maximize it, you must double-click on it or invoke its Control menu using

Alt-Spacebar, then select the option you desire. (To bypass the Control menu, see "Alt-Tab" below.) Following is a sequential set of directions for using Alt-Esc.

To Switch Application Windows Using Alt-Esc

1. From anywhere within Windows, press Alt-Esc. The next application in sequence will become selected. If the current application is an icon, the Windows desktop will appear and the icon will be selected.
2. Make the next applications in sequence active by continuing to hold down the Alt key and repeatedly pressing the Esc key.
3. When the application you wish to switch to is selected, release the Alt-Esc keys.

ALT-TAB

Alt-Tab will make the currently active window inactive, move to the next window in sequence, and make it active. The sequence is determined by the order in which the programs were first invoked.

When you switch to an application icon using Alt-Tab, the icon becomes selected and is automatically restored to the state it was in before it was minimized. This eliminates the need to invoke the icon's Control menu and select Restore.

To Switch Application Windows Using Alt-Tab

1. From anywhere within Windows, press Alt-Tab. The next application in sequence will become selected.
2. Continue to hold down the Alt key, and repeatedly press the Tab key, until the application you desire is selected.
3. Make the selected application active by releasing the Alt-Tab keys. If the selected application is currently an icon, it will automatically be restored to its original state on the desktop.

TASK LIST

Task List is a utility program that is available at all times while Windows is running. Its purpose is to help you organize and control all the currently executing applications (called tasks). Using Task List, you can switch to any program, stop a program from running (or end a task), arrange the application icons at the bottom of the Windows desktop, or arrange all the open windows on the desktop in a logical and accessible way.

The Task List can be invoked at any time by pressing Ctrl-Esc, or by double-clicking in any blank area of the Windows desktop. (Do not double-click on any window or icon.) Task List is a dialog box, depicted in Figure 2.1.

SWITCHING TO A TASK

• EXPLANATION Switching to a task causes the currently active task to become inactive, and the new, selected task to become active.

To Use the Mouse

1. Invoke Task List by pressing Ctrl-Esc, or by double-clicking anywhere on the Windows desktop. Task List will appear, with a list box of the currently executing applications within it.

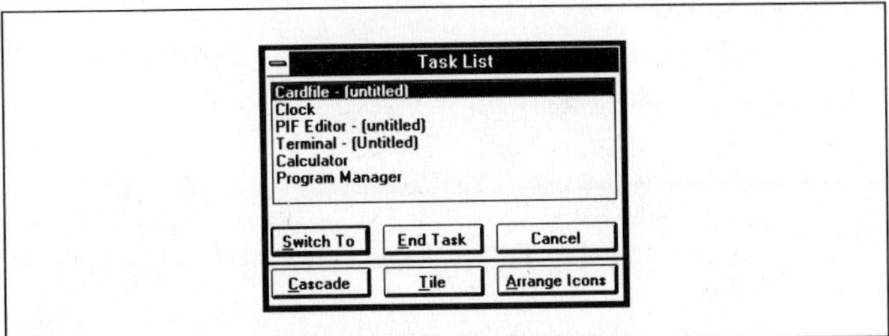

Figure 2.1: Task List

2. Click on the name of the application you want to switch to, then click on Switch To. An alternate way of doing this is simply to double-click on the name of the application to which you want to switch.

To Use the Keyboard

1. Invoke the Task List by pressing Ctrl-Esc. Task List will appear, with a list box of the currently executing applications within it.
2. Use ↑ or ↓ to select the application to which you want to switch.
3. Select Switch To by pressing ↵, or by pressing Alt-S.

See Also The Key Commands

ENDING A TASK

Ending a task will stop an application from executing. The application, and anything it is currently working on, will be eliminated from the Windows desktop. If the work the application is doing has not been saved to disk, that work will be lost.

You should only choose to end a task when the task has permanently halted and will not respond to any keyboard or mouse actions. Most of the time, the programs that malfunction in this way are DOS applications executing under Windows. *Invoking End Task should be a last resort.* If you can't close a malfunctioning DOS application using End Task, try terminating it (see "Terminating a DOS Application").

To Use the Mouse

1. Invoke Task List by pressing Ctrl-Esc, or by double-clicking anywhere on the Windows desktop. Task List will appear, with a list box of the currently executing applications within it.
2. Click on the name of the application you want to end, then click on End Task.

To Use the Keyboard

1. Invoke Task List by pressing Ctrl-Esc. Task List will appear, with a list box of the currently executing applications within it.
2. Use ↑ or ↓ to select the application you want to end.
3. Select End Task by pressing Alt-E.

See Also Terminating a DOS Application

TERMINATING A DOS APPLICATION

• **EXPLANATION** Sometimes DOS applications malfunction when they run under Windows. This is especially true of older DOS applications and ones that try to directly control the display adaptor or hard disk. When a DOS application will no longer respond to keyboard or mouse input of any kind, and you can not close it by selecting End Task from Task List, you can choose to terminate it. This is done by switching from the application to the Windows desktop, then using the application's Control menu to select the Terminate option.

Once a DOS program has been terminated, there is a distinct possibility that Windows could become unstable. Before you terminate a program, it is strongly advised that you close all active windows. Once the program is terminated, exit Windows and reboot your computer.

To Use the Mouse

1. With the malfunctioning DOS program on the screen, press Alt-Esc to switch back to the Windows desktop.
2. Close all executing Windows programs. Save all open data files to disk.

3. Select the program icon of the malfunctioning DOS program by clicking on it; its Control Menu will appear.
4. Select Settings. A dialog box will appear. This box allows you to adjust various settings for DOS programs that execute under Windows.
5. Select Terminate. You will see a warning dialog box that advises you to reboot your computer once you have terminated the application.
6. Select OK.

To Use the Keyboard

1. With the malfunctioning DOS program on the screen, press Alt-Esc to switch back to the Windows desktop.
2. Close all executing Windows programs. Save all open data files to disk.
3. Select the program icon of the malfunctioning DOS program by holding down the Alt key and pressing Esc repeatedly, until the icon is highlighted.
4. Press Alt-Spacebar. The icon's Control menu will appear.
5. Select Settings by typing **T**. A dialog box will appear. This box allows you to adjust various settings for DOS programs that execute under Windows.
6. Select Terminate by typing **T**. You will see a warning dialog box that advises you to reboot your computer once you have terminated the application.
7. Press Tab to highlight the OK button, then press ↵.

ARRANGING APPLICATION ICONS

• **EXPLANATION** In working with Windows, application icons sometimes get scattered all over the desktop. They are frequently hidden by windows. Using Task List, you can bring all the application icons down to the bottom of the desktop and arrange them in one neat row.

To Use the Mouse

1. Invoke Task List by pressing Ctrl-Esc, or by double-clicking anywhere on the Windows desktop. Task List will appear, with a list box of the currently executing applications within it.
2. Select Arrange Icons. Task List will disappear, and all the application icons will appear at the bottom of the desktop.

To Use the Keyboard

1. Invoke Task List by pressing Ctrl-Esc. Task List will appear, with a list box of the currently executing applications within it.
2. Select Arrange Icons by pressing Alt-A. Task List will disappear, and all the application icons will appear at the bottom of the desktop.

See Also The Key Commands

TILING AND CASCADING APPLICATION WINDOWS

• **EXPLANATION** If you open more than two application windows at a time, the Windows desktop can get crowded; it becomes difficult to see which windows are open. To solve this problem, the Task List utility has two commands--Cascade Windows and Tile Windows--that automatically size and place application windows.

When open applications are displayed in a cascade, they overlap each other, with only one window visible—the one that was active when Cascade was selected (see Figure 2.2).

When open application windows are tiled, the space on the Windows desktop is evenly divided among the windows; they are arranged on the screen so they don't overlap. At least some portion of the program area of each group is visible (see Figure 2.3).

Before selecting either Cascade Windows or Tile Windows, make sure the windows that you want to arrange are open.

See Also Arranging Multiple Group Windows—Tile and Cascade (Ch.1)

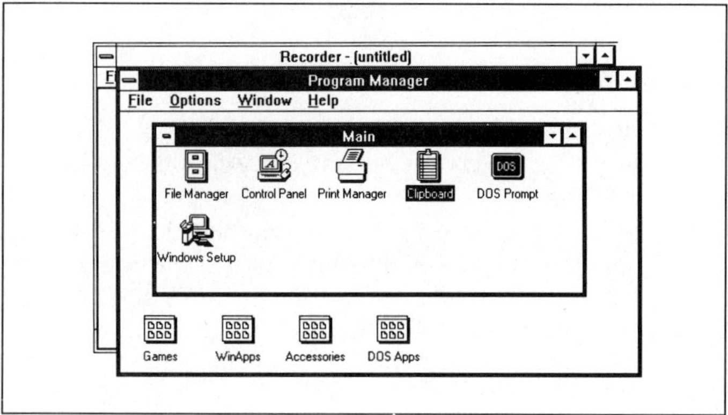

Figure 2.2: Application windows in a cascade

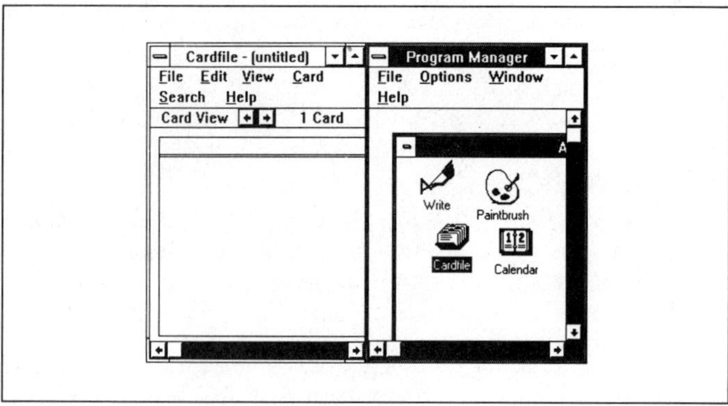

Figure 2.3: Tiled application windows

To Cascade Windows

Mouse

1. Invoke Task List by pressing Ctrl-Esc, or by double-clicking anywhere on the Windows desktop. Task List will appear, with a list box of the currently executing applications within it.
2. Select Cascade. Task List will disappear, and all open application windows will appear in a cascade.

Keyboard

1. Invoke Task List by pressing Ctrl-Esc. Task List will appear, with a list box of the currently executing applications within it.
2. Select Cascade by pressing Alt-C. Task List will disappear, and all open application windows will appear in a cascade.

To Tile Windows

Mouse

1. Invoke Task List by pressing Ctrl-Esc, or by double-clicking anywhere on the Windows desktop. Task List will appear, with a list box of the currently executing applications within it.
2. Select Tile. Task List will disappear, and all open application windows will appear tiled.

Keyboard

1. Invoke the Task List by pressing Ctrl-Esc. Task List will appear, with a list box of the currently executing applications within it.
2. Select Tile by pressing Alt-T. Task List will disappear, and all open application windows will appear tiled.

Chapter 3

WINDOWS HELP

To aid you in understanding and using Windows, Microsoft has provided one of the most advanced help facilities available, called simply Windows Help. Help does not appear as a Program Item icon in a Group Window. Instead, Windows Help is accessible at any time from within almost every Windows program.

Windows Help is always used in conjunction with an application-specific Help text file supplied by the application developer. Most Help text files are divided into four general sections: Index, Keyboard, Commands, and Procedures. Some programs have additional sections, or sections with different names.

The Windows Help screen is divided into two parts. The upper part of the screen contains a set of *navigation buttons,* which aid you in moving through the Help text; see Figure 3.1. The lower part is the Help window's workspace.

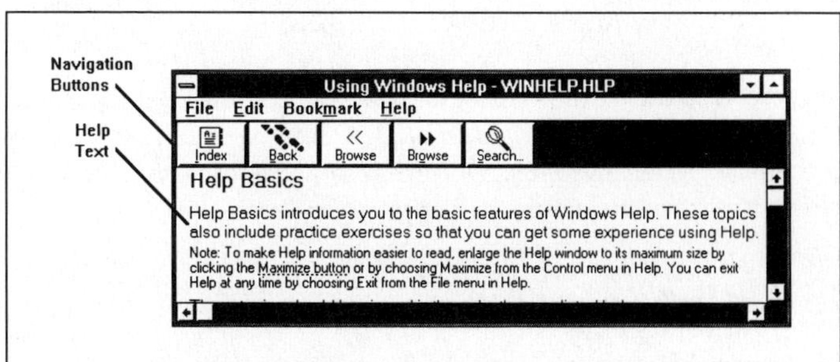

Figure 3.1: A standard help screen

INVOKING HELP

• EXPLANATION There are four methods for invoking Help: pull down the active application's Help menu and select an option; click on a Help Command button in a dialog box, if available; press the F1 key; or press the Shift-F1 key sequence. Shift-F1 and Help Command buttons are only available under certain circumstances, as explained below.

To Use the Mouse

There are two ways to invoke the Help system using the mouse: by accessing the currently active program's menu system, or by using a Help Command button in a dialog box.

The Menu System

- Pull down the Help menu and click on the desired menu option. Windows Help will run, the Help text file for the currently active program will be loaded into it, and the Help program will go directly to the portion of the Help text file you specified—Index, Procedures, etc.

Dialog Boxes Some dialog boxes have a Help Command button. To access Windows Help through a Command button, click on the button. Windows Help will run and Help text concerning the currently active dialog box will appear.

To Use the Keyboard

There are three ways to invoke the Help system using the keyboard: using the menu system, using the F1 key, and using the F1 or Shift-F1 key sequences.

The Menu System

1. Press Alt-H. The program window's Help menu will drop down.

2. Use the direction keys to move between menu options. When the option you want is highlighted, press ↵. Another keyboard method is to select a menu option by pressing its key letter (the highlighted letter in the option). The result of either method is that Windows Help will run, the Help text file for the currently active program will be loaded into it, and the Help will go directly to the portion of the text file you specified—Index, Procedures, etc.

The F1 and Shift-F1 Keys Press the F1 key at any point when you are working with an application and Windows Help will display the Help Index file for that program. There are certain times when the F1 key won't work (when there is no Help text file for a given program, when a menu is pulled down, or while a dialog box is active). Some dialog boxes have Help Command buttons in them, which are explained above.

Some Windows programs implement an advanced Help feature in which you hold down the Shift and F1 keys, and a question mark appears beside the mouse pointer. You can then move the mouse pointer/question mark around on the screen and select a menu option or press a key sequence, and the Help text for that specific option or sequence will appear. None of the applications that are included with Windows use this feature.

ACCESSING THE INDEX

• EXPLANATION Most Windows Help Indexes have three main headings under which Help topics are organized: Keyboard, Commands, and Procedures. Individual programs may have more headings or headings with different names. Under each heading, program-specific topics are listed alphabetically.

The following text describes how to access the Help Index from inside Windows Help. You can jump to the Help Index directly from an application's Help menu. This is described in "Invoking Help."

Whether you are working with a mouse or the keyboard, the Help Index is always accessed using the Index button. See Figure 3.2.

To Use the Mouse

- Place the mouse pointer over the Index button and click. The current Help text file's Index will appear.

To Use the Keyboard

- Press Alt-I to activate the Index button. The current Help text file's Index will appear.

Figure 3.2: The Index button

JUMPING TO A REFERENCE

• EXPLANATION Some of the text that appears in the Windows Help workspace is underlined, either with a solid line or a dotted line. If you are using a color monitor, it is also green. The text that is underlined with a solid line is a *reference*, or a word or phrase for which there is further explanatory Help text. Place the mouse pointer over the reference and click, and Windows Help will jump to the text that describes the reference.

To Use the Mouse

1. Place the mouse pointer over the reference. The pointer will change from an arrow shape to a picture of a hand with the index finger pointing.
2. Click the left mouse button. Windows Help will jump to the text that describes the reference.

READING A DEFINITION

• **EXPLANATION** Some of the text that appears in the Windows Help workspace is underlined with a dotted line. If you are using a color monitor, it is also green. The dotted underline means that definitions for the underlined text are available.

To Use the Mouse

1. Place the mouse pointer over the underlined text. The pointer will change from an arrow shape to a picture of a hand with the index finger pointing.
2. Click the left mouse button and hold it down. A definition for the underlined word or phrase will appear.
3. When you have read the definition, release the mouse button.

BROWSING

• **EXPLANATION** Browse will move through the current Help text file screen by screen, at the heading level from which it starts.

Whether you are working with a mouse or the keyboard, browsing is always accomplished using the Browse buttons. See Figure 3.3.

To Browse Forward

To Use the Mouse Start from anywhere in the Help system that you like, except at the last screen at the current heading level.

- Click on the Forward Browse button, which is the one with double arrows pointing to the right. Windows Help will move to the next Help screen at the current heading level.

To Use the Keyboard Start from anywhere in the Help system that you like, except at the last screen at the current heading level.

- Press Alt-O. Windows Help will move to the next Help screen at the current heading level.

To Browse in Reverse

To Use the Mouse Start from anywhere in the Help system that you like, except at the first screen at the current heading level.

- Click on the Reverse Browse button, which is the one with double-arrows pointing to the left. Windows Help will move to the previous Help screen at the current heading level.

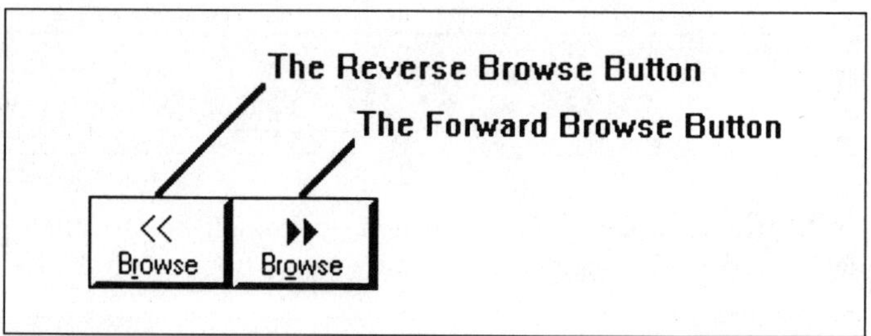

Figure 3.3: The Browse buttons

To Use the Keyboard Start from anywhere in the Help system that you like, except at the first screen at the current heading level.

- Press Alt-R. Windows Help will move to the previous Help screen at the current heading level.

MOVING BACKWARD

• EXPLANATION Windows Help keeps a record of where you have been, so that you can move back along the path you have traveled. This is accomplished by using the Back button. See Figure 3.4.

To Use the Mouse

Start from anywhere in the Help system that you want, except at the very first screen that appears when you invoke Help. (You can't move backward if you have not moved forward yet.)

- Click on the Back button. Windows Help will move to the Help screen that appeared prior to the current one.

To Use the Keyboard

Start from anywhere in the Help system that you want, except at the very first screen that appears when you invoke Help.

- Press Alt-B. Windows Help will move to the Help screen that appeared prior to the current one.

Figure 3.4: The Back button

SEARCHING ON A KEYWORD

• **EXPLANATION** Windows Help has a search facility that allows you to search the current Help text file for specific words or phrases. This is accomplished via the Search button. See Figure 3.5.

Once invoked, the Search button brings up the Search dialog box pictured in Figure 3.6.

To Use the Mouse

Start from anywhere in the Windows Help program.

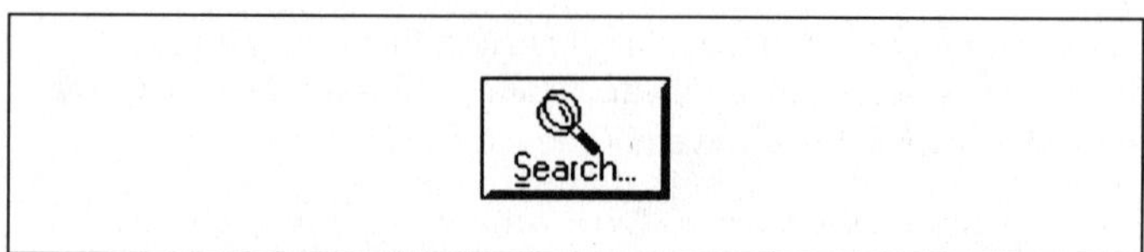

Figure 3.5: The Search button

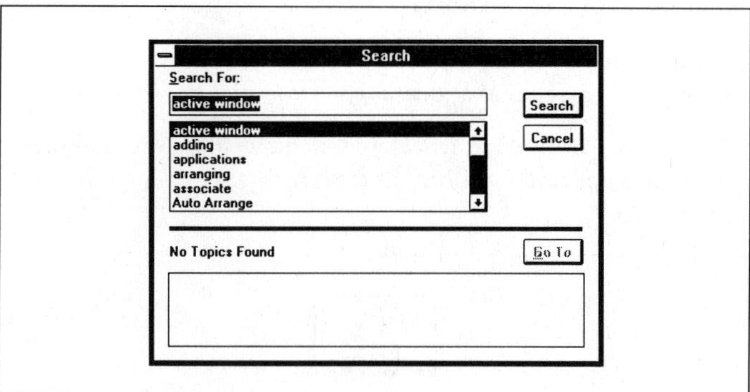

Figure 3.6: The Search dialog box

1. Click on the Search button. The Search dialog box will appear. Within the Search dialog box is a text box and two list boxes. One list box is filled with keywords, which are common words or phrases for which Windows users often search. The text box is where you type in the keyword for which you wish to search. By default, it contains the first word in the keyword list box.
2. Press Backspace to delete the word currently in the text box.
3. Type in the word or phrase for which you wish to search. As you type, Windows Help will move through the list of keywords, displaying the word that most closely matches what you are typing. If the word you are searching on appears in the list box, you can simply click the mouse pointer on it, rather than continue typing it.
4. Click on the Search Command button. The Help topics that contain the specified keyword will appear in the lower list box.
5. Click on the topic you wish to see.
6. Click on Go To. The Help text that contains your search keyword will appear.
7. Close Windows Help.

PRINTING HELP TEXT

• **EXPLANATION** Windows Help gives you the ability to print the Help text for the current heading.

To Use the Mouse

Start with the Help text you wish to print displayed on the screen.

- Pull down the File menu and select Print.

To Use the Keyboard

Start with the Help text you wish to print displayed on the screen.

1. Press Alt-F.
2. Type **P**.

CREATING A BOOKMARK

• **EXPLANATION** A *bookmark* in Windows Help terminology is a location marker placed at any point in the Windows Help text file. Markers are given names, which appear under the Bookmark menu and are numbered sequentially starting with 1. Click on a bookmark's name and Windows Help will take you to the specified point in the current Help text file.

To Use the Mouse

Start from the Help text screen that you wish to mark.

1. Pull down the Bookmark menu and select Define. You will see a dialog box with a text box and a list box inside it. The text box is where you type the name of the bookmark. By default, the bookmark name is the same as the heading of your current location in the Help text file.
2. If necessary, press Backspace to delete the current bookmark name.
3. Type the bookmark name you desire.
4. Click on the OK Command button. The bookmark you created will appear under the Bookmark menu. To go to the text specified by a bookmark, pull down the Bookmark menu and select the desired bookmark.

DELETING A BOOKMARK

• **EXPLANATION** Once you have used a bookmark a few times, you will probably memorize its subject matter and no longer need it. At that point, you can delete the bookmark.

To Use the Mouse

Start from anywhere in Windows Help, but make sure the Help text file containing the bookmark you wish to delete is loaded.

1. Pull down the Bookmark menu and select Define. You will see a dialog box with a text box and a list box inside it. The list box contains a list of the currently defined bookmarks.
2. Click on the name of the bookmark you wish to delete.
3. Click on the Delete Command button. The bookmark you specified will be deleted.

Chapter 4

THE CLIPBOARD

The Windows Clipboard is a temporary storage location reserved for graphic or textual data. You can transfer data from any program into the Clipboard and then copy that data into a different program.

Data is copied to and from the Clipboard using the Cut, Copy, or Paste menu options in the Edit menu. Almost every Windows program has an Edit menu. Those programs that don't have one, such as Windows Clock, are so simple that they don't need access to the Clipboard.

You can also cut or paste data from DOS applications into the Clipboard. If the DOS program is running in full-screen mode, you must copy the full screen into the Clipboard. Also, you can paste textual data into non-windowed applications, but not graphic data.

Windows is shipped with a utility program, also called Clipboard, which allows you to view and delete any Clipboard data. Using the Clipboard program, you can save the contents of the Clipboard to file and retrieve them later. Use of the Clipboard program is explained in this chapter, along with use of the Clipboard itself.

CUTTING OR COPYING DATA INTO THE CLIPBOARD

• **EXPLANATION** Before you can cut or copy data, you must select it by telling the application program with which you are working what program information you want placed in the Clipboard. This is done differently in different programs. Consult the Help text file for the program you are using to learn how to select data for that program.

The following instructions apply generally to most Windows programs. Certain programs may access the Clipboard in a different way.

To Use the Mouse

- With the data you wish to cut or copy selected, pull down the Edit menu and select Cut or Copy. If you choose Cut, the selected data will be copied into the Clipboard and be deleted from whatever program you are using. If you select Copy, it will not be deleted.

To Use the Keyboard

To Cut

- With the data you wish to cut or copy selected, press Shift-Del.

To Copy

- With the data you wish to cut or copy selected, press Ctrl-Insert.

COPYING DATA FROM A WINDOWED DOS PROGRAM

• EXPLANATION A windowed DOS program is a standard MS-DOS program that appears inside a window. Windows will run windowed DOS programs only when it is operating in 386 Enhanced mode. The window used for windowed DOS programs does not have a menu bar. It has only one menu—the Control menu—and all copying and pasting is done from there. Though you can copy data, you cannot cut data from a windowed DOS application.

The Control menu option that allows you to cut and paste from DOS programs is called Edit. Selecting Edit brings up a cascading menu that has Copy, Paste, Mark, and Scroll options; this menu is shown in Figure 4.1.

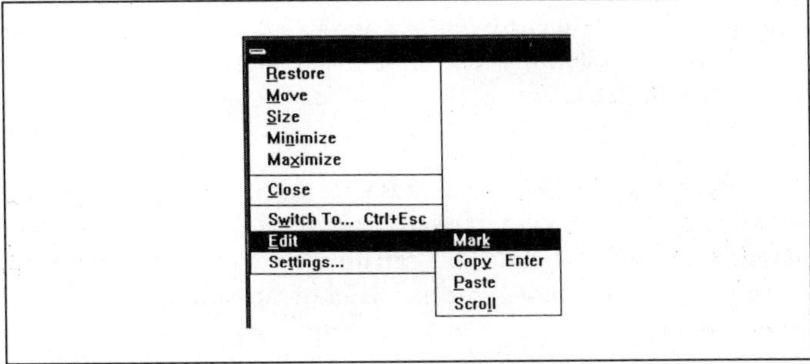

Figure 4.1: The open Edit menu with cascade

To Use the Mouse

Start with the windowed DOS program you wish to work with on the screen.

1. Place the mouse pointer at the upper-left corner of the onscreen information you wish to copy. Click the left mouse button, hold it down, and drag the mouse pointer to the lower-right corner of the onscreen information you wish to copy.
2. Release the mouse button.
3. Pull down the Control menu and select Edit.
4. Select Copy.

COPYING DATA FROM A NON-WINDOWED DOS PROGRAM

• EXPLANATION A non-windowed DOS program is a standard MS-DOS program that runs under Windows, but takes up the entire screen. In Windows parlance, the program is running in "full-screen mode." Outwardly, it looks like a standard DOS application and there is no evidence that Windows is present at all. To switch back to Windows, you press special key sequences (Alt-Tab or Alt-Esc).

You can copy data from one of these full-screen DOS programs, but you must copy the entire screen. You cannot cut data from a non-windowed DOS program; you can only copy it. Also, because the Windows mouse pointer is unavailable when a DOS program is operating in full-screen mode, all copying is done using key sequences.

To Use the Keyboard

Start with the DOS program you wish to work with on the screen.

- Press PrtScrn. On newer keyboards, the key is labeled Print Screen. If you try this and it doesn't work, it may be because you have an older keyboard. Try Alt-PrtScrn or Shift-PrtScrn.

Notes You normally can't copy graphics from full-screen DOS programs running under Windows; you can only copy text.

COPYING WINDOWS SCREENS INTO THE CLIPBOARD

• **EXPLANATION** Windows 3.0 comes with a built-in screen-capture facility. You can, at any time, press a key sequence and capture the entire current Windows desktop in the Clipboard. You can press a different key sequence and capture only the currently active Window.

The data captured in this way is stored in the form of a bit map. It can be pasted into Windows Paintbrush workspace and edited and then saved as a Windows 3.0 bit map (.BMP extension) or as a PC Paintbrush file (.PCX extension). The latter file format is understood by a wide variety of programs.

To Use the Keyboard

Start by positioning the windows you wish to capture. Make them look exactly the way you want by sizing and moving them.

- Press PrtScrn and the entire Windows desktop—open windows, icons, everything—will be copied into the Clipboard. Press Alt-PrtScrn if you want only the currently active window to be copied into the Clipboard.

Notes The Windows screen-capture facility is useful, but it has some pitfalls. You cannot, for example, use the Alt-PrtScrn combination to capture the image of a window with a menu pulled down. The moment you touch the Alt key, Windows assumes you are going to pull down a different menu, and closes the one that is currently on screen. You have to capture the entire desktop to get an image of a pulled-down menu.

PASTING DATA FROM THE CLIPBOARD

• EXPLANATION To paste data from the Clipboard into a program means that you copy data that has been stored temporarily in the Clipboard into a program. You can paste textual or graphic data into any program that supports the type of data being transferred.

Pasting data into a Windows program does not delete the data from the Clipboard. There are only two ways to delete data from the Clipboard: use the Clipboard viewing program to delete it (see "Deleting Clipboard Data"), or overwrite it by cutting or copying new data into the Clipboard.

The following instructions apply generally to most Windows programs. Certain programs may access the Clipboard in a different way.

To Use the Mouse

Start by making sure the data you wish to paste is in the Clipboard. See "Running the Clipboard Program" in this chapter.

1. With the data you wish to paste residing in the Clipboard, pull down the Edit menu.
2. Select Paste.

To Use the Keyboard

- With the data you wish to paste in the Clipboard, press Shift-Insert.

PASTING DATA INTO A WINDOWED DOS PROGRAM

• EXPLANATION Pasting data into a windowed DOS program is very similar to pasting data into a Windows program, with one notable exception: you can only paste unformatted textual data into a windowed DOS program (or a non-windowed one for that matter).

To Use the Mouse

Start by making sure the data you wish to paste is in the Clipboard. See "Running the Clipboard Program" in this chapter.

1. From within the DOS program, position the cursor at the point where you wish the text pasted.
2. With the data you wish to paste residing in the Clipboard, pull down the Control menu.
3. Select Edit. A cascaded submenu will appear.
4. From the cascaded submenu, select Paste.

PASTING DATA INTO A NON-WINDOWED DOS PROGRAM

• EXPLANATION Windows has no facility for allowing you to paste text into a non-windowed DOS application while it is on screen. Instead, you have to shrink the full-screen DOS program to an icon and then select the Paste option from its Control menu.

To Use the Mouse

Start by making sure the data you wish to paste is in the Clipboard. See "Running the Clipboard Program" in this chapter.

1. Run the DOS program into which you are going to paste data. Position the cursor *exactly* at the point where you want the pasted text to appear.
2. Press Alt-Esc to switch back to the Windows desktop. The non-windowed DOS application will be reduced to an icon, which will appear at the bottom of the desktop screen.
3. Click on the DOS program's icon once. The program's Control menu will appear.
4. Select Edit. A cascaded submenu will appear.
5. From the cascaded submenu, select Paste. Windows will copy text out of the Clipboard and into the DOS application. From the application's perspective, it will be just as if the text were typed at the keyboard.

UNDOING A CUT OR PASTE

• **EXPLANATION** Once you have cut or pasted data to or from a Windows program, you may see that you have made a mistake. Most Windows programs offer you an Undo option, which will delete the most current Cut or Paste command and return the workspace to the state it was in before the command was executed. Some standard DOS programs offer their own form of Undo, but the procedures described below are for Windows programs only.

These instructions assume that you have just cut or pasted a text or graphic, and that you wish to undo what you have done. They apply generally to most Windows programs.

To Use the Mouse

- Pull down the Edit menu and select Undo. The window's workspace will revert to the way it was before you executed the Cut or Paste command.

RUNNING THE CLIPBOARD PROGRAM

• EXPLANATION You can view the contents of the Clipboard at any time by running the Clipboard program. You can also use the Clipboard program to delete the contents of the Clipboard, change the format in which data is displayed by the Clipboard program, save the Clipboard's contents to a file, or retrieve a file containing Clipboard data.

To Use the Mouse

Start by cutting or copying some data into the Clipboard. See "Cutting or Copying Data into the Clipboard."

1. Place the mouse pointer over the Clipboard icon, pictured in Figure 4.2

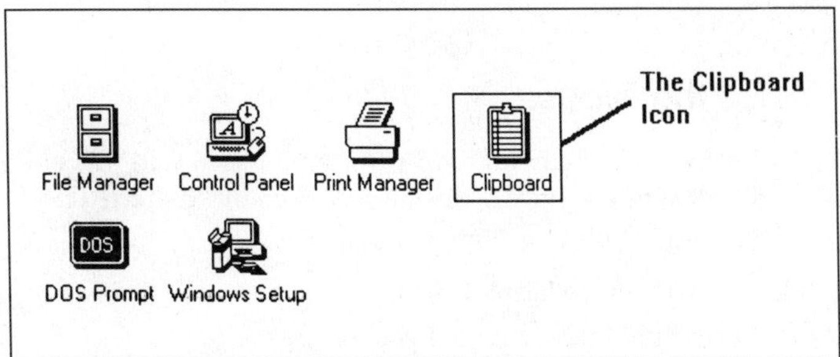

Figure 4.2: The Clipboard icon

2. Double-click on the icon to run the Clipboard program. When the program runs, whatever data is in the Clipboard will be visible immediately in the Clipboard program's workspace.

CHANGING THE DATA DISPLAY FORMAT

• **EXPLANATION** From the Clipboard program, you can change the format in which Clipboard data is displayed. This is accomplished using the Display menu.

The Clipboard program divides text into three display formats: Text, OEM Text, and Owner Display. Text is the standard alphanumeric text available from the keyboard. When displaying in Text mode, the Clipboard program translates any IBM extended characters into standard text. To see IBM extended characters—lines, corners, shading—you need to switch to OEM Text. Switching to OEM Text also turns any proportionally spaced font into non-proportionally spaced Courier font.

The Owner Display format will display the text in its original font and format. The program from which you cut the text must be a Windows program, and it must still be active, either as a window or an icon, for Owner Display to be available. If the originating program is not active, Owner Display will not appear as a menu option.

To Use the Mouse

Start by running the Clipboard program, which will place the Clipboard window on the desktop. Make sure there is text in the Clipboard, not a bit map or a picture.

1. Pull down the Display menu.
2. Select the Display format you wish.

DELETING CLIPBOARD DATA

• **EXPLANATION** Once you have finished using the Clipboard to move data between programs, it is a good idea to delete that data from the Clipboard. This frees up memory that Windows can use.

To Use the Mouse

Start with some kind of data in the Clipboard.

1. From the Main program group, run the Clipboard program by double-clicking on the Clipboard icon.
2. Pull down the Edit menu.
3. Select Delete. A dialog box will appear, asking you to confirm the deletion.
4. Select OK.

Notes If you have data stored in the Clipboard that you think you may need, you can save it in a file and load it back into the Clipboard later. See "Saving Clipboard's Contents" and "Retrieving Clipboard's Contents," below.

SAVING CLIPBOARD'S CONTENTS

• **EXPLANATION** Because the Clipboard is often used to transfer important data, you may wish to save the Clipboard's contents as a file. Clipboard files have a .CLP extension.

To Use the Mouse

Start with some kind of data in the Clipboard.

1. From the Main program group, run the Clipboard program by double-clicking on the Clipboard icon.
2. Pull down the File menu and select Save As. A dialog box that lists all of the Clipboard files in the current directory will appear. There will be a text box in which you are supposed to enter the name of the Clipboard file. It will have the default file name, DEFAULT.CLP, in it.
3. Key in a name for the Clipboard file, or accept the default name.
4. Select OK.

RETRIEVING CLIPBOARD'S CONTENTS

• **EXPLANATION** Data that appears in the Clipboard can be stored in Clipboard files, which by default have a .CLP extension. When the time comes to use data that has been saved in a file, you can use the Clipboard program to retrieve the file. The Clipboard program will retrieve only .CLP files.

To Use the Mouse

1. From the Main program group, run the Clipboard program by double-clicking on the Clipboard icon.
2. Pull down the File menu and select Open. A dialog box that lists all of the Clipboard files in the current directory will appear.
3. Select the name of the Clipboard file you wish to retrieve.
4. Select OK.

Chapter 5

THE FILE MANAGER

Windows 3.0 provides a program for manipulating files, called File Manager. File Manager presents you with a visual representation of all the disks and files in your system. When File Manager runs, a window similar to the one in Figure 5.1 appears.

As you can see, the File Manager uses document windows. (See Chapter 1, "The Program Manager" for an explanation of document windows.) The directory structure for the hard disk appears in a single document window called Directory Tree. File Manager displays only one Directory Tree at a time; it will not display multiple Directory Trees side by side. When the time comes to view lists of files, they will appear in additional document windows called *directory windows*. Such windows are named with the directory whose files are listed in the window (for example, C:\DOS*.*).

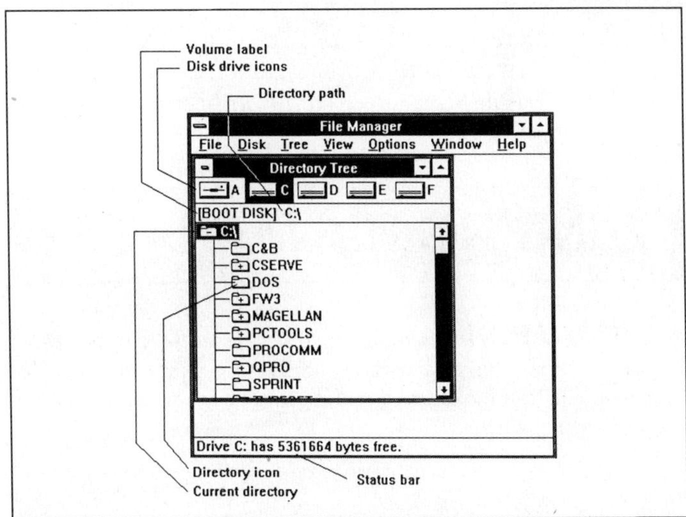

Figure 5.1: The File Manager Opening Screen

From a directory window, you can select one or more files and change their attributes, move them between directories, or open, print, rename, delete, or copy them. Figure 5.2 shows two open directory windows that could be used in this manner.

Figure 5.2 also shows the Directory Tree in the form of a document icon at the bottom of the File Manager workspace. Any document windows in File Manager can be minimized to a document icon.

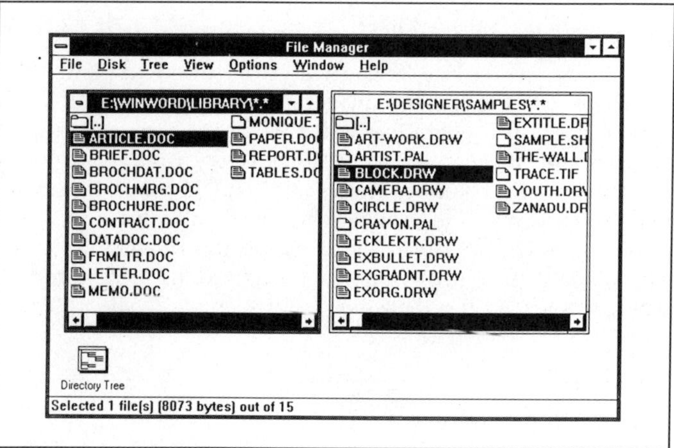

Figure 5.2: The File Manager screen with directory windows displayed

RUNNING FILE MANAGER

• **EXPLANATION** File Manager is an essential component of Windows, and is run just like any other Windows program. The File Manager icon is in the Main program group. It is a picture of a filing cabinet; see Figure 5.3.

To Use the Mouse

To run File Manager, start from the Main program window.

1. Place the mouse pointer over the File Manager icon.
2. Double-click the left mouse button. The File Manager window will appear.

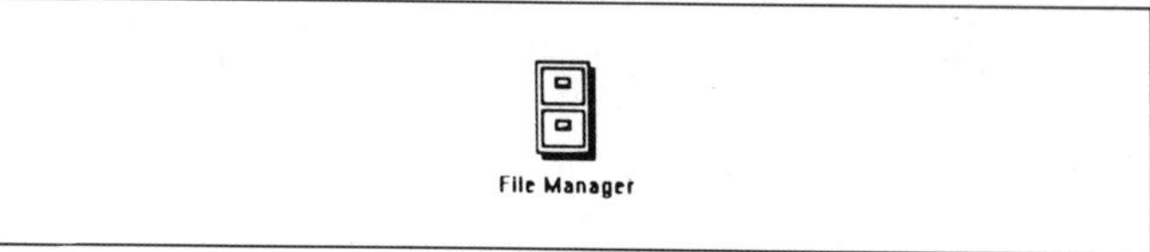

Figure 5.3: The File Manager icon

CLOSING FILE MANAGER

• EXPLANATION As you work with File Manager, you may use the View or Options menus to change certain settings within it. When you close File Manager, it gives you the option of saving these settings.

To Use the Mouse

1. Pull down File Manager's Control menu.
2. Select Close. The confirming dialog box will appear.
3. Select the Save Settings check box if you wish to preserve the settings of the View and Options menus.
4. Click on OK.

CHANGING DISK DRIVES

• EXPLANATION File Manager's Directory Tree window will only display one disk structure or directory tree at a time. For this reason, File Manager allows you to specify which disk drive Directory Tree addresses—it allows you to switch drives.

To Use the Mouse

1. Place the mouse pointer over the icon of the drive to which you wish to switch.
2. Click on the icon.

To Use the Keyboard

- Press Ctrl-*Drive*. Remember, *Drive* specifies a drive letter of your choosing.

CHANGING DIRECTORIES

• EXPLANATION Part of working with the Directory Tree involves selecting and using different directories. To change directories, you must ensure that the icon is visible in the Directory Tree window. (See "Expanding Directory Tree," below.)

Before you can change directories, the Directory Tree window must be open and active.

To Use the Mouse

1. Use the directory scroll bar to make the directory icon you wish to switch visible.
2. Place the mouse pointer over the icon of the directory to which you wish to switch.
3. Click on the icon.

To Use the Keyboard

There are several methods for navigating the directory tree using the keyboard. The following list is *not* sequential; rather, each item listed simply describes a different method for using the keyboard to move around the directory tree.

- Press ↑ or ↓ to move from directory icon to directory icon.
- To move up and down the directory tree a screen at a time, press PgUp or PgDn.
- To jump directly to a directory, press the first letter of the directory. If you wanted to switch to the ZEBRA directory, for example, you would press Z.

EXPANDING DIRECTORY TREE

• EXPLANATION The File Manager displays directory structures in the form of an "inverted tree" diagram, in the Directory Tree window. Each subdirectory is represented by the symbol of a folder. Some "branches" of the tree—subdirectories—may not be visible. This is not because they've scrolled off the bottom of the window; it's because the File Manager has collapsed those branches in order to make the tree as a whole easier to view. Directories that have subdirectories beneath them have a minus sign in them. Directories that have subdirectories beneath them that are not visible have a plus sign in them.

You can make subdirectories visible by expanding one level of a branch on the tree, an entire branch, or the entire tree. There is a difference between expanding one level and expanding a branch. The former displays only those folders immediately below the highlighted folder. The latter displays *all* directories below the highlighted folder.

To Expand One Level

Mouse

1. Change to the directory you wish to expand.
2. Pull down the Tree menu.
3. Select Expand Branch

These three steps are combined into one when you use the mouse: clicking on a directory folder also expands it.

Keyboard

1. Change to the directory you wish to expand.
2. Press the plus key (+).

To Expand the Entire Branch

Mouse

1. Change to the directory whose branch you wish to expand.
2. Pull down the Tree menu.
3. Select Expand Branch.

Keyboard

1. Change to the directory you wish to expand.
2. Press the asterisk (*).

To Expand the Entire Tree

You can expand the entire directory tree from anywhere in the directory structure. You don't have to be at any particular level in the tree.

Mouse

1. Pull down the Tree menu.
2. Select Expand All.

Keyboard

- Press and hold the Ctrl key, then press the asterisk (Ctrl-*).

COLLAPSING A DIRECTORY TREE

• EXPLANATION The File Manager allows you to "collapse" a directory so that you see only the directory levels you want. When a tree or a branch of a tree is collapsed, the directories beneath the current directory disappear from the screen, and the symbol inside the current directory's icon changes from a minus sign to a plus sign.

To Use the Mouse

1. Select the directory icon in the level directly above the directory icons you no longer wish to see.
2. Pull down the Tree menu.
3. Select Collapse Branch.

These three steps are combined into one when using the mouse. Clicking on a folder with a minus sign collapses everything beneath the folder into the folder.

To Use the Keyboard

1. Select the directory icon in the level directly above the directory icons you no longer wish to see.
2. Press the minus key (–).

OPENING A DIRECTORY WINDOW

To work with directory windows, the user must first know how to open them, or make them appear in the File Manager workspace. This is accomplished by double-clicking on the directory icon.

To Use the Mouse

- Place the mouse pointer over the directory icon of the directory you wish to view, and double-click the left mouse button. A directory window containing a list of files in the specified directory will appear.

To Use the Keyboard

1. Use the direction keys to select the directory you wish to view.
2. Press ↵.

CLOSING A DIRECTORY WINDOW

• **EXPLANATION** Closing a directory window is very similar to closing a standard program window. The mouse action is exactly the same, while the key command is slightly different.

To Use the Mouse

- Pull down the window's Control menu and select Close.

To Use the Keyboard

- Press Ctrl-F4.

Notes Directory windows are a specific type of window called document windows. The key sequence described above is the same for all document windows, not just directory windows.

SELECTING THE ACTIVE DIRECTORY WINDOW

• EXPLANATION Only one directory window can be active at a time. The active directory window is the one with which you are working. Its title bar is the same color as File Manager's title bar; the inactive window's title bar is some alternate color.

To Use the Mouse

- Place the mouse pointer on the Directory window you wish to make active, and click.

To Use the Keyboard

1. Press and hold the Ctrl key, then press Tab repeatedly until the window you want is active. This will make each directory window active in succession.
2. When the directory window you wish to switch to is selected, release the Ctrl and Tab keys.

CASCADING DIRECTORY WINDOWS

● **EXPLANATION** When open directory windows are displayed in a cascade, they overlap each other. Only the contents of the first window are visible; the title bars of the other windows can be seen behind it. A cascade of windows is shown in Figure 5.4. Before selecting Cascade, make sure the directory windows that you want to arrange are open.

To Use the Mouse

- Pull down the Window menu of the File Manager and select Cascade.

To Use the Keyboard

- Press Shift-F5.

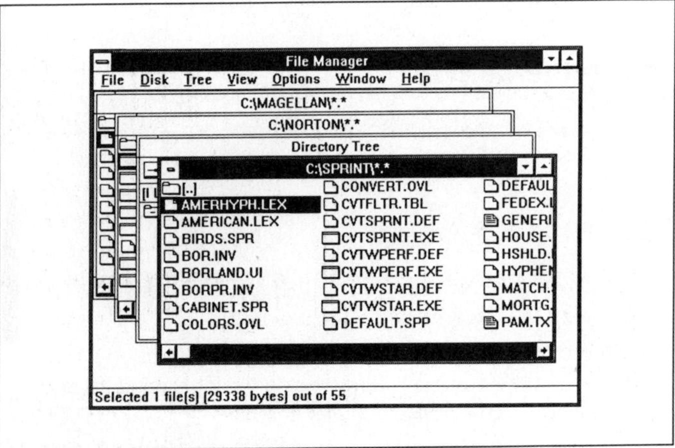

Figure 5.4: Directory windows in a cascade

TILING DIRECTORY WINDOWS

• EXPLANATION When open directory windows are tiled, the workspace provided by the File Manager is evenly divided among the directory windows. The windows are arranged on screen so they don't overlap. At least some portion of the workspace area of each group is visible. Before selecting Tile, make sure the directory windows that you want to arrange are open.

To Use the Mouse

1. Pull down the Window menu of the File Manager.
2. Select Tile.

To Use the Keyboard

- Press Shift-F4.

SELECTING A FILE

• EXPLANATION To select a file is to highlight it, which tells the File Manager to make it the object of whatever action you next initiate. You can select multiple files and perform actions on them. A selected file appears in reverse video, as shown in Figure 5.5.

Every directory window has at least one file selected. When the directory window opens, the first file in the file list is selected.

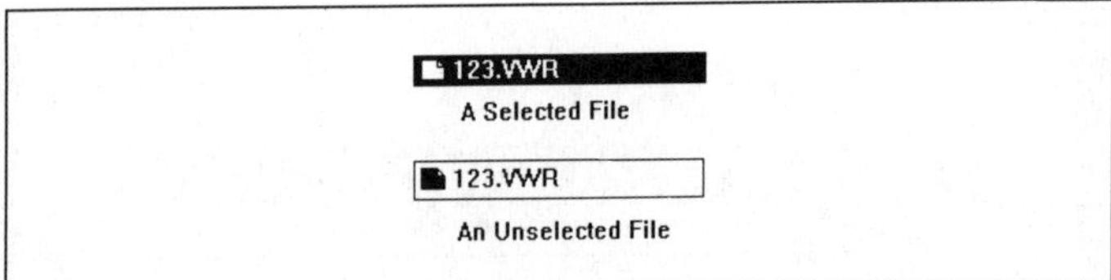

Figure 5.5: A selected and an unselected file

To Use the Mouse

- Place the mouse pointer over the file you wish to select, and click.

To Use the Keyboard

- Use the direction keys to move the selection cursor from file name to file name.

See Also Selecting Multiple Files

SELECTING MULTIPLE FILES

• EXPLANATION File Manager allows you to select entire groups of files and perform operations on them. You can select groups of consecutive files, which are files that appear one after the other in the directory window list; or you can select non-consecutive groups of files, such as the fourth, the tenth, then the fourteenth file in the list. To select multiple files, start with an open directory window in front of you.

To Select Consecutive Files with the Mouse

1. Place the mouse pointer over the first file in the consecutive series and select the file by clicking.
2. Move the mouse pointer to the last file in the series.

3. Hold down the Shift key and then press the left mouse button. All the files between the current one and the one previously selected will become selected files.

Notes This comes in handy when you want to select ranges of files, or when you want to select every file in the directory. Press Ctrl-/ to select all files in a window.

To Select Non-consecutive Files with the Mouse

1. Place the mouse pointer over the first file you wish to select, and click.
2. Move the mouse pointer over the next file.
3. Hold down the Ctrl key, then click the left mouse button.
4. Move the mouse pointer to the next file and repeat the Ctrl-click operation.
5. Repeat this operation for every file you wish to select.

Notes This is useful when you need to scroll through a large number of files and select only some of them.

See Also Copying or Moving a File

RENAMING A FILE

• EXPLANATION File Manager lets you rename any file, as long as the new name follows DOS file-naming conventions.

To Use the Mouse

Start with an open directory window that contains the file you want to rename.

1. Place the mouse pointer over the file name and select the file.
2. Pull down the File menu.
3. Select Rename. A dialog box will appear. It will contain the name of the file you just selected, along with an empty text box where you will key in the new file name.
4. Type the new file name.
5. Click on Rename.

Notes You can rename a group of files by selecting them and invoking the renaming procedure described above. When the Rename dialog box appears, instead of keying in a single file name, type a wildcard specification. For example, if you select ten files that end with a .PCX extension, you can rename them all so that they have a .BAK extension. When the Rename dialog box appears, simply type *.BAK and press ↵.

DELETING A FILE

• EXPLANATION File Manager lets you delete any file on any disk. The exception to this is network disk drives, where your privilege level may restrict you.

To Use the Mouse

Start with an open directory window that contains the file you want to delete.

1. Place the mouse pointer over the name of the file you wish to delete, and click.
2. Pull down the File menu.
3. Select Delete. A dialog box will ask you to confirm the deletion.

4. Click on Delete. A new dialog box will appear, containing a more strident warning and again asking you to confirm the deletion of the file.
5. Click on Yes.

Notes You can turn off the last confirmation dialog box by pulling down the Options menu, and selecting Confirmation. When a dialog box comes up, click on the Confirm On Delete check box.

You can delete a group of files by selecting them and invoking the deletion procedure described above. When the Delete dialog box appears, you will see the name of every file you selected in a text box. If there are more names than can fit in the box, they will simply disappear past the edge of the text box.

RUNNING A PROGRAM FROM FILE MANAGER

• EXPLANATION The File Manager is not just a tool for organizing and copying files; you can also use it to run programs. This is accomplished by displaying the program's file name in a directory window, and then opening it by double-clicking on it. Windows treats three file types as programs, those with an .EXE, .COM, or .BAT extension. Start by making sure that a directory window for the directory that contains the program file you wish to run is on screen.

To Use the Mouse

- Place the mouse pointer over the program's file name and double-click. The program will run. If it is a DOS program, it will run in full-screen mode.

To Use the Keyboard

1. Use the direction keys to select the file.
2. Press ↵. The program will run. If it is a DOS program, it will run in full-screen mode.

See Also Creating a Program Icon

ASSOCIATING A FILE WITH AN APPLICATION

• EXPLANATION To associate a file is to link all files with a specific extension to a specific program file. If you are using MultiMate, for instance, you can tell File Manager that all files that end in .DOC (which is the file extension for MultiMate documents) are associated with the program file MM.EXE. From that point on, when you open or double-click on any .DOC file, MultiMate will automatically run and load the specified file.

To Use the Mouse

1. Select the file whose extension you wish to associate.
2. Pull down the File menu and select Associate. A dialog box will appear, asking you to key in the name of the program file.
3. Type the full path and file names of the program file.
4. Press ↵.

Notes It is important to key in the complete path name and program file name. For example, if the program file were MultiMate's (MM.EXE), and it resided in the WPROC directory of the C drive, you would type C:\WPROC\MM.EXE.

COPYING OR MOVING A FILE

• **EXPLANATION** The File Manager lets you copy or move files in a very simple, visual way that is far superior to the standard DOS command line. You simply place the directory window that is the source of the file on screen. Then, you "drag" the file from that window to its destination—either another open directory window, a directory folder on the Directory Tree, or a drive icon.

To Use the Mouse

Start by making sure the destination directory, whether it's a directory window or a directory folder, is visible on the File Manager workspace.

1. Open the directory window for the source and destination directory.
2. Select the file or files you wish to copy or move.
3. If you are copying a file, press the Ctrl key and hold it down.
4. Place the mouse pointer over the selected file. If more than one file is selected, place it over any file in the group.
5. Click the left mouse button and hold it down. This "grabs" the selected file(s).
6. Move the pointer onto the destination directory window or directory folder.
7. Release the Ctrl key and mouse button if you are copying a file, or the mouse button if you are moving a file. A dialog box will appear, asking you to confirm that you want the files copied or moved, as appropriate.
8. Click on Yes. Additional dialog boxes will appear if there are files in the destination directory that have the same name as the files you are copying or moving.

Notes If the source and destination directories are on different drives, click and hold the left button once to copy, and use Alt-Click to move.

CREATING A PROGRAM ICON

• EXPLANATION The File Manager and Program Manager are designed to interact so that you can create a program icon in a very easy, visual way. The process is similar to that of copying or moving files, except that in this case you "move" a program file directly from the File Manager into a Group Window of the Program Manager.

To Use the Mouse

1. Place the File Manager and Program Manager windows on the desktop at the same time.
2. Size them so that they each take up half of the desktop. You might want to tile them using the Task List (see Chapter 2, "Switching between Windows").
3. In the Program Manager, open the Group Window that will contain the program icon.
4. In the File Manager, open the directory window that contains the program file name.
5. Select the program file for which you wish to create an icon.
6. Place the mouse pointer over the selected file.
7. Click the left mouse button and hold it down; this "grabs" the selected file.
8. Move the pointer out of the File Manager, across the Windows desktop, into the Program Manager, and into the destination Group Window.

9. Release the mouse button. An icon for the selected program will appear. If the program is a standard DOS program, the icon will be a gray box with the word *DOS* in it.

See Also Adding a Program to a Group (Ch. 1)

Chapter 6

SETTING UP AND CONFIGURING WINDOWS

THE SETUP PROGRAM

Setup is a program that allows you to reconfigure Windows for a new type of display, keyboard, mouse, or local area network (LAN). As you reconfigure Windows, Setup will request that you insert some of the original Windows installation disks in the computer's floppy disk drive, so keep the disks handy. After you use Setup to reconfigure Windows, you must exit Windows and then restart it for the change to take effect. You can also use Setup to install standard DOS applications into the Windows environment.

When Setup is run from within the Windows environment, it functions as a Windows program; it has a program icon, uses menus and dialog boxes, and does everything you would expect. When you run Setup from the DOS command line, it comes up in character mode and displays the same screens and prompts used when you installed Windows for the first time. Setup operates in this character-based mode for two reasons. First, if Windows is currently installed for a graphics display that is not present, you can use character-mode Setup to reconfigure Windows for the current display. Second, you can install a device driver that was not shipped with Windows, or an updated version of a device driver that has already been installed.

It is beyond the scope of this reference guide to document character-based Setup. For more information, consult your Windows Users Guide, under "Running Setup from MS-DOS."

RUNNING SETUP

• **EXPLANATION** Setup is a Windows program. Its icon is located in the Main program group. When Setup is first run, the window depicted in Figure 6.1 appears.

The workspace in Setup simply displays the current system configuration; you can't interact with it in any way. For that, you use the Options menu.

To Use the Mouse

1. Open the Main program group.
2. Double-click on the Setup icon, which is a picture of a computer with an open box of software in front of it. The Setup window will appear.

CHANGING THE DISPLAY

• **EXPLANATION** When you replace your current video display with a new type of display, you need to reconfigure Windows to use the new display. This is accomplished using Setup.

To Use the Mouse

1. Run the Setup program. (See "Running Setup" above for instructions.)
2. Pull down the Options menu.

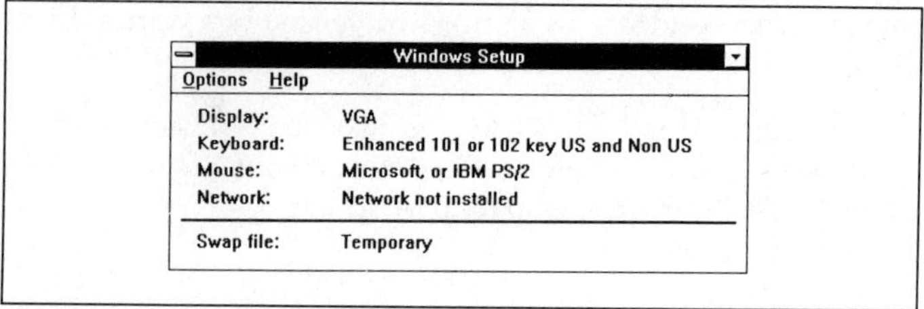

Figure 6.1: The Setup window

3. Select Change System Settings. A dialog box that contains four drop-down list boxes will appear.
4. Click on the arrow pointing downward on the right side of the Display drop-down list box. A list of video displays will appear.
5. Use the scroll bar to move through the list and select the new video display.
6. Click on OK. A dialog box will appear, asking you to insert one of the original Windows disks.
7. Insert the specified disk in the floppy disk drive, then click on OK. A dialog box with two icons inside it will appear. One icon will be a picture of several overlapping Windows, the other will be a picture of a DOS prompt. The Windows icon will shut down the current Windows session and start a new one. The DOS prompt icon will shut down the current Windows session and return you to DOS.
8. Select the desired icon. When Windows restarts, it will expect to find the video display you specified.

Notes If you have already installed Windows for the type of display selected in step 5, the display driver may already be on the hard disk, in which case Setup will not prompt you for a Windows installation disk.

CHANGING THE KEYBOARD

• EXPLANATION There may be times when you need to change the type of keyboard in use. This may happen because you upgrade to a newer keyboard, or because you switch to a computer that uses an unusual type of keyboard.

To Use the Mouse

1. Run the Setup program. (See "Running Setup" at the beginning of this chapter for instructions.)
2. Pull down the Options menu.
3. Select Change System Settings. A dialog box that contains four drop-down list boxes will appear.

4. Click on the arrow pointing downward on the right side of the Keyboard drop-down list box. A list of keyboards will appear.
5. Use the scroll bar to move through the list and select the new keyboard.
6. Click on OK. A dialog box with two icons inside it will appear. One icon will be a picture of several overlapping Windows, the other will be a picture of a DOS prompt. The Windows icon will shut down the current Windows session and start a new one. The DOS prompt icon will shut down the current Windows session and return you to DOS.
7. Select the desired icon. When Windows restarts, it will expect to find the keyboard you specified.

CHANGING THE MOUSE

• EXPLANATION If you change the type of mouse you are using, you need to reconfigure Windows so that it knows of this change.

To Use the Mouse

1. Run the Setup program. (See "Running Setup" at the beginning of this chapter.
2. Pull down the Options menu.
3. Select Change System Settings. A dialog box that contains four drop-down list boxes will appear.
4. Click on the arrow pointing downward on the right side of the Mouse drop-down list box. A list of pointing devices will appear.
5. Use the scroll bar to move through the list and select the new mouse.
6. Click on OK. A dialog box will appear, asking you to insert one of the original Windows disks.
7. Insert the specified disk in the floppy disk drive, then click on OK. A dialog box with two icons inside it will appear.

One icon will be a picture of several overlapping Windows, the other will be a picture of a DOS prompt. The Windows icon will shut down the current Windows session and start a new one. The DOS prompt icon will shut down the current Windows session and return you to DOS.

8. Select the desired icon. When Windows restarts, it will expect to find the mouse display you specified.

Notes If you have installed Windows for this type of mouse before, the mouse driver may already be on the hard disk, in which case Setup will not prompt you for a Windows installation disk.

CHANGING A NETWORK

• EXPLANATION If your PC is modified to interact with a local area network (LAN), you will need to reconfigure Windows so that it knows what type of network is available.

To Use the Mouse

1. Run the Setup program. (See "Running Setup" at the beginning of this chapter for instructions.)
2. Pull down the Options menu.
3. Select Change System Settings. A dialog box that contains four drop-down list boxes will appear.
4. Click on the arrow pointing downward on the right side of the Network drop-down list box. A list of networks will appear.
5. Use the scroll bar to move through the list and select the new network.
6. Click on OK. A dialog box will appear, asking you to insert one of the original Windows disks.
7. Insert the specified disk in the floppy disk drive, then click on OK. Windows may or may not ask you to insert more disks.
8. Repeat step 7 if you are prompted to insert additional disks. Once all the necessary files have been copied to the Windows directory, a dialog box with two icons inside it

will appear. One icon will be a picture of several overlapping Windows, the other will be a picture of a DOS prompt. The Windows icon will shut down the current Windows session and start a new one. The DOS prompt icon will shut down the current Windows session and return you to DOS.

9. Select the desired icon. When Windows restarts, it will expect to find the network you specified present in the system.

Notes If you have installed Windows for this type of network before, the network driver may already be on the hard disk, in which case Setup will not prompt you for any Windows installation disks.

SETTING UP NON-WINDOWS APPLICATIONS

• EXPLANATION One of Setup's most advanced features is its ability to easily set up applications to work in the Windows environment. Setup does this by scanning all the hard disks in your computer system and looking for programs it recognizes. (Setup recognizes most major PC applications, though there are a few that it does not know.)

After scanning the hard disk, Setup creates a list of the applications it recognizes. It presents that list in a dialog box and gives you the option of adding one, a few, or all of the applications to the Windows environment. Setup then creates a program group for the applications and places program icons for them in the new group.

To Use the Mouse

1. Run the Setup program. (See "Running Setup" at the beginning of this chapter for instuctions.)
2. Pull down the Options menu.
3. Select Setup Applications. A dialog box that contains a drop-down list will appear. The drop-down list box allows you to specify which hard disk drives to scan for applications.

4. Click on the arrow pointing downward on the right side of the drop-down list box to see a list of available drives.
5. Select the drive you wish to scan by clicking on it; to accept the default value of *ALL DRIVES*, go to step 6.
6. Click on OK. Setup will scan the specified drives for applications. When the scan is complete, you will see a screen similar to the one in Figure 6.2.
7. Select the applications you wish to add to Windows by clicking on their names in the Applications list box. You can select multiple applications. If you select an application and then choose not to add it, unselect it by clicking on its name again. If you want to add all the applications listed, you don't have to select any of them. Just click on the Add All command button.
8. Click on the Add command button. If you add one or more applications and then change your mind, remove them by selecting them from the Setup For Use dialog box and then clicking on the Remove command button.
9. Click on OK. Setup will add the selected programs to the Program Manager. If you selected Windows applications, it will add them to the Windows Applications program group; if you selected standard DOS programs, it will add them to the Non-Windows Applications program group. If neither of these groups exists, Setup will create them.

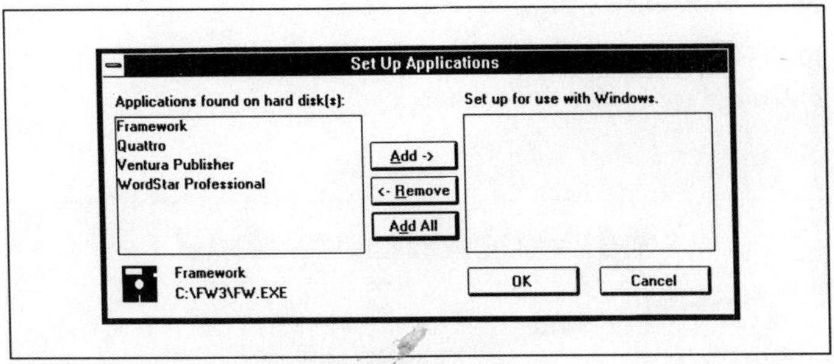

Figure 6.2: The Setup Applications dialog box

THE CONTROL PANEL

The Control Panel is a utility program that lets you configure Windows in many ways. Using the Control Panel, you can change the default printer and printer port, install a new printer driver, install new fonts, customize the mouse, or change the time and date. You can also do some fun things, like permanently change the colors that Windows uses, or use a graphic image generated in Paintbrush as a backdrop for the Windows desktop.

All of the above procedures are described in the following pages. Because of space considerations, there are some things that the Control Panel can do that are not described in this chapter. They are: configuring a serial port, setting international currency and number formats, setting the keyboard speed, turning the warning beep on or off, and setting options for Windows 386 Enhanced mode.

The Control Panel is a Windows program, so naturally it has a program icon. The Control Panel program icon looks like a desktop computer with a mouse attached and a clock above it. It is located in the Main program group. Run the Control Panel just as you would any other Windows program. (See "Opening a Window" in Chapter 1.) The Control Panel is unlike most other Windows programs. Its workspace doesn't contain a blank area for graphics or text. Rather, it contains a number of icons that represent options within the Control Panel; see Figure 6.3.

If you are not running Windows in 386 Enhanced Mode, the 386 Enhanced mode icon does not appear.

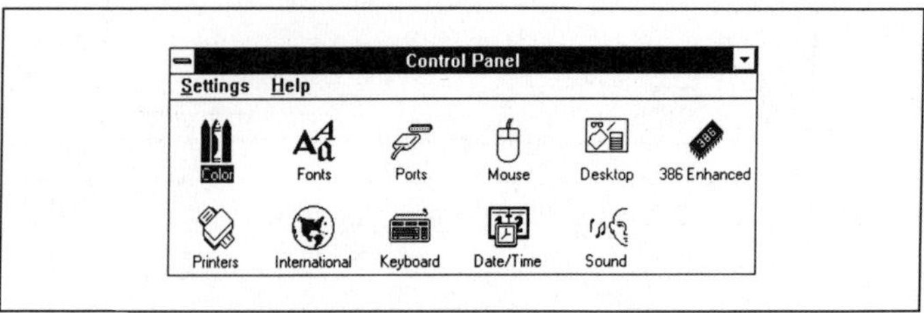

Figure 6.3: The Control Panel window

RUNNING A CONTROL PANEL OPTION

• **EXPLANATION** There are two ways to invoke a Control Panel option: by using an option's icon, or by pulling down the Settings menu and selecting the name of the option.

To Use the Mouse

1. Place the mouse pointer over the icon of the option you wish to invoke.
2. Click the mouse twice in rapid succession.

To Use the Keyboard

1. Press Alt-S to pull down the Settings menu.
2. Use the direction keys to select the option you wish to invoke.
3. Press ↵.

Notes Each Control Panel option, when invoked, produces a window of some kind. Unlike the document windows produced by other programs, the windows generated by the Control Panel can be closed with the standard key sequence for closing a window (Alt-F4), not the key sequence that closes document windows (Ctrl-F4).

CHANGING WINDOWS' COLOR SCHEME

• **EXPLANATION** A *color scheme* is the series of colors assigned to the component parts—borders, title bars, etc.—of the Windows environment. After installation, Windows comes up in a default color scheme composed of grays, whites, and blues. Included with Windows are ten other color schemes. You can switch to one of these schemes using the Control Panel.

To Use the Mouse

1. Run the Colors option. (See "Running a Control Panel Option.") The Colors icon is a picture of several upright

crayons. A dialog box will appear. There will be a drop-down list box in the upper portion of the box.

2. Click on the arrow pointing downward at the right edge of the drop-down list box. A list of alternate color schemes will appear.
3. Click on the scheme of your choice. The lower portion of the dialog box will display the new color scheme.
4. Click on OK.

You aren't limited to the color schemes in the list. To assign any other color in the color palette to any element of the environment, run the Colors option, click on Color Palette, click on the element whose color you want to change, and click on the color of your choice in the Basic Colors palette.

CHANGING THE DESKTOP PATTERN

• EXPLANATION Windows offers you the ability to overlay the Windows desktop with a graphic pattern. The Control Panel has several stored patterns, along with an editor that lets you create custom patterns.

To Use the Mouse

1. Run the Desktop option. (See "Running a Control Panel Option.") The Desktop icon is a gray square with a yellow folder and a pair of glasses on it. A dialog box will appear. There will be a drop-down list box labeled *Pattern* in the upper portion of the box.
2. Click on the arrow pointing downward at the right edge of the Pattern drop-down list box. A list of patterns will appear.
3. Click on the pattern of your choice.
4. Click on OK.

Notes If you have both a desktop pattern and a wallpaper graphic active (see "Changing the Desktop Wallpaper"), the wallpaper will take precedence. You will see the pattern only where the wallpaper is not visible. To edit the pattern you have selected, click on the Edit Pattern command button before you click on OK.

CHANGING THE DESKTOP WALLPAPER

• EXPLANATION Windows offers you the ability to change the Windows desktop from a single color to a graphic image. The images are stored in a bitmap file of the type produced by Windows Paintbrush. (Bitmap files have a .BMP extension). Windows has several stored bitmap files that can be used as wallpaper.

To Use the Mouse

1. Run the Desktop option. (See "Running a Control Panel Option.") The Desktop icon is a gray square with a yellow folder and a pair of glasses on it. A dialog box will appear. There will be a drop-down list box labeled *Wallpaper* in the center of the box.
2. Click on the arrow pointing downward at the right edge of the Wallpaper drop-down list box. A list of .BMP files will appear.
3. Click on the file of your choice.
4. Click on OK.

Notes Windows comes with several bitmap files, but not all are useful as desktop backgrounds. One way to assemble a collection of bitmap files is to look for graphic files with a .PCX extension, which are produced by ZSoft's PC Paintbrush program. .PCX files are common; most graphics programs either import or export .PCX files. Once you have a .PCX file, you can use Windows Paintbrush to convert it to a .BMP file.

CHANGING THE SIZING GRID

• EXPLANATION The sizing grid is an invisible series of horizontal and vertical lines with which icons and windows will align themselves if you so specify. When Windows first starts, you are able to place icons anywhere on the screen that you like. This can be confusing because they often overlap each other or end up scattered randomly around the desktop. Once the sizing grid is active, icons and windows will "snap" to (move to and line up with) the nearest grid line.

To Use the Mouse

1. Run the Desktop option. (See "Running a Control Panel Option.") The Desktop icon is a gray square with a yellow folder and a pair of glasses on it. A dialog box will appear. There will be a box in the lower-right corner labeled *Sizing Grid.* Within it will be two scroll boxes labeled *Granularity* and *Border Width.*
2. Click on the up or down arrow of the Granularity scroll box. The numbers in the box will scroll up or down. The maximum number is 49 and the minimum is zero. Each additional number value expands the grid by eight pixels. A value of zero turns the grid off.
3. Click on OK.

CHANGING THE BORDER WIDTH

• **EXPLANATION** The Control Panel allows you to change the border width of all the windows on the desktop.

To Use the Mouse

1. Run the Desktop option. (See "Running a Control Panel Option.") The Desktop icon is a gray square with a yellow folder and a pair of glasses on it. A dialog box will appear. There will be a box in the lower-right corner labeled *Sizing Grid.* Within it will be two scroll boxes labeled *Granularity* and *Border Width.*
2. Click on the up or down arrow of the Border Width scroll box. The numbers in the box will scroll up or down. The maximum number is 49 and the minimum is one. Each additional number value expands the border by eight pixels.
3. Click on OK.

INSTALLING A NEW PRINTER

• **EXPLANATION** If you change printers, or get an additional printer, you will need to prepare Windows to access and use your new device. This involves using the Control Panel to "tell" Windows about the new printer and to copy a special configuration file, called a *printer driver*, onto your hard disk. You will need your original Windows installation disks for this procedure.

To Use the Mouse

1. Run the Printers option. (See "Running a Control Panel Option.") The Printers icon is a small picture of a laser printer. The Printers dialog box will appear.
2. Click on the Add Printer command button. The dialog box will expand until it appears similar to the one in Figure 6.4.
3. Scroll through the list of printers until yours appears, then click on it.
4. Click on Install. A dialog box will appear, asking you to insert a specific Windows installation disk in the floppy disk drive.
5. Insert the disk in the floppy disk drive, then click on OK.

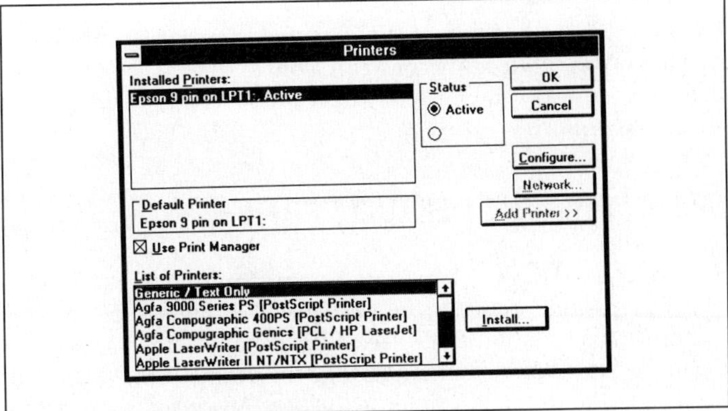

Figure 6.4: The Printers dialog box with list box

SELECTING A PRINTER PORT

• EXPLANATION Your computer has two types of output ports, parallel and serial. The standard DOS machine can have up to three parallel ports and four serial ports, though most computers have only one of each. If you switch your printer from one port to another, you need to use the Control Panel to configure Windows so that it knows it will find the printer on that port.

To Use the Mouse

1. Run the Printers option. (See "Running a Control Panel Option.") The Printers icon is a small picture of a laser printer. The Printers dialog box will appear.
2. Make sure that the printer that is on the new port is selected. If it is not, then select it by moving the mouse pointer over the printer name and clicking.
3. Click on the Configure command button. The Printers-Configure dialog box will appear. In it will be a list box labeled *Ports*.
4. From the Ports list box, select the new printer port.
5. Click on OK.
6. When the Printers dialog box reappears, click on OK.

Notes Windows does not check to see if a port exists when you specify it. You could easily configure your system to print to a port that does not exist; this has no effect (nothing gets printed), and should be avoided.

SWITCHING THE DEFAULT PRINTER

• EXPLANATION Windows automatically uses one printer, called the default printer. If you have installed multiple printers for Windows, you will at times need to make a different printer the default printer. Before you can change the default printer, you will need to make the new printer active; see "Switching the Active Printer."

To Use the Mouse

1. Run the Printers option. (See "Running a Control Panel Option.") The Printers icon is a small picture of a laser printer. The Printers dialog box will appear.
2. Move the mouse pointer over the list of installed printers and double-click on the printer you wish to make the default. The name of the default printer, listed in the Default Printer box, will change.
3. Click on OK.

SWITCHING THE ACTIVE PRINTER

• **EXPLANATION** If you install more than one printer on the same port, Windows automatically makes one active—able to access the port—and one inactive. When you install a new printer or change default printers, you need to make the new printer active before you can use it.

To Use the Mouse

1. Run the Printers option. (See "Running a Control Panel Option.") The Printers icon is a small picture of a laser printer. The Printers dialog box will appear.
2. Move the mouse pointer over the Installed Printers box and click on the printer you wish to make active.
3. Click on the Active option button.
4. Click on OK.

Notes Windows will not let you make a printer active if it is configured to use an output port that is already in use by an active printer. You must make the output port available by making the printer that uses it inactive, before you can activate the current printer.

Each port can have multiple printers configured for it, though only one of them can be designated as active. The default printer must be active.

INSTALLING A FONT

• EXPLANATION A font is a graphically rendered image of a particular typeface. Fonts are named after the typefaces they represent—Courier, Times Roman, Helvetica, etc. Windows uses a type of font called a screen font to display typefaces on screen. Windows is shipped with an adequate number of screen fonts for most tasks, but certain users of Windows will find that they need additional ones. The Control Panel allows you to add screen fonts to the Windows environment.

When you are adding a screen font, you must have a disk with the new font files on it, or the new files must be somewhere on your hard disk.

To Use the Mouse

1. Run the Fonts option. (See "Running a Control Panel Option.") The Fonts icon is a picture of three letter As. The Fonts dialog box will appear.
2. Click on the Add command button. The Add Fonts dialog box will appear.
3. Place the disk containing the new font files in the floppy disk drive.
4. Use the Directories list box to select the floppy disk drive, usually drive A. If the font files are stored on the hard disk, select the directory they are stored in. The names of the fonts on the floppy disk will appear in the Font Files list box.
5. Move the mouse pointer over the Font Files list box and click on the name of the font file you wish to add.
6. Click on OK.
7. When the Fonts dialog box reappears, click on OK.

REMOVING A FONT

• EXPLANATION The Control Panel allows you to remove fonts from the Windows environment. You may want to do this if you have too many fonts installed, or if your fonts are taking up too much hard disk space.

To Use the Mouse

1. Run the Fonts option. (See "Running a Control Panel Option.") The Fonts icon is a picture of three letter As. The Fonts dialog box will appear.
2. Move the mouse pointer over the Installed Fonts list box and click on the font you wish to remove.
3. Click on the Remove command. The Remove Fonts dialog box will appear, asking you to confirm the font deletion.
4. Click on Yes.
5. When the Fonts dialog box reappears, click on OK.

CHANGING THE TIME AND DATE

• **EXPLANATION** Windows uses your computer's internal clock to keep track of the time and date. You can use the Control Panel to change the time and date settings.

To Use the Mouse

1. Run the Date/Time option. (See "Running a Control Panel Option.") The Date/Time icon is a picture of a desk calendar with a clock in front of it. The Date/Time dialog box will appear. There will be two miniature scroll boxes in it, one labeled date and one labeled time.
2. Click on the up or down scroll arrow for each scroll box to change the setting. You can also click on the displayed date or time and a cursor will appear. Then you can key in the time or date value directly.
3. Click on OK.

Notes When Windows changes the time and date, it not only modifies the software clock maintained by MS-DOS, it also changes the time and date in the battery-maintained CMOS RAM clock on your computer's mainboard. This means that when the computer is turned off and back on again, the correct time and date will have been maintained. It also means that you don't have to use a CMOS RAM setup program to change settings in your computer's clock. You can use Windows.

SWAPPING MOUSE BUTTONS

• **EXPLANATION** Under Windows, the left mouse button is the primary mouse button. This enables a right-handed person to easily move the mouse and click with his or her right index finger. Left-handed people often find this arrangement bothersome, so Windows lets you change the right mouse button to the primary button.

To Use the Mouse

1. Run the Mouse option. (See "Running a Control Panel Option.") The Mouse icon is a picture of a mouse. The Mouse dialog box will appear.
2. Click on the Swap Left/Right Mouse button check box. The moment you click on this check box, the mouse button switches. So now you have to use the right mouse button to get out of the Mouse dialog box.
3. Click on OK.

ADJUSTING THE MOUSE TRACKING SPEED

• **EXPLANATION** The tracking speed is the rate at which the mouse pointer moves across the Windows screen, relative to the distance the mouse is moved across the table. If the tracking is set to slow, you must move the mouse further on the table to make the pointer move the same distance across the screen. Different tracking speeds are comfortable for different people, so the Control Panel allows you to adjust the rate.

To Use the Mouse

1. Run the Mouse option. (See "Running a Control Panel Option.") The Mouse icon is a picture of a mouse. The Mouse dialog box will appear.

2. Click on the Mouse Tracking Speed scroll bar to change the tracking speed. The moment you click on this scroll bar, the change takes effect. If you make the speed too slow, the pointer will seem like it is not responding to the mouse. Move the mouse slowly and adjust the speed upward.
3. Click on OK.

ADJUSTING THE DOUBLE-CLICK SPEED

• **EXPLANATION** The double-click speed is the period of time between the two clicks that comprise a double-click. If the double-click rate is fast, you must click very quickly for Windows to accept the double-click. If the double-click rate is slow, you can click at a more deliberate pace and Windows will accept the double-click.

To Use the Mouse

1. Run the Mouse option. (See "Running a Control Panel Option.") The Mouse icon is a picture of a mouse. The Mouse dialog box will appear.
2. Click on the Double Click Speed scroll bar to change the double-click rate. The moment you click on this scroll bar, the change takes effect.
3. Move the mouse pointer over the TEST box and double-click. If the box becomes highlighted (or if an already highlighted box returns to normal video), the double-click was successful.
4. Move between the Double Click Speed scroll bar and the TEST box, adjusting and testing the double-click rate until it suits you.
5. Click on OK.

Chapter 7

THE PRINT MANAGER

The Print Manager is a Windows program that automatically manages all printing done by Windows applications. When you direct a Windows application to print information, the application then formats the information for the default printer and stores it in a *print file,* which is then passed to the Print Manager.

The Print Manager accepts print files from Windows applications and sends them to the printer. It can accept multiple print files, prioritize them, and send them to the printer one after the other. A group of print files waiting to be printed is called the *print queue.* Using the Print Manager you can change the order of the queue, delete print files from the queue, or pause and resume printing.

The Print Manager window is somewhat similar to the Help window because it too has command buttons located below the menu bar but above the workspace. See Figure 7.1.

When a file is in the queue and being printed, it is listed at the top of the Print Manager workspace with a small picture of a printer next to it. The next file in the list has a numeral two next to it, indicating it is the second file in the queue. The next file has a numeral three, and so on. Information on the size of the print file and the time it was submitted to the Print Manager appears along

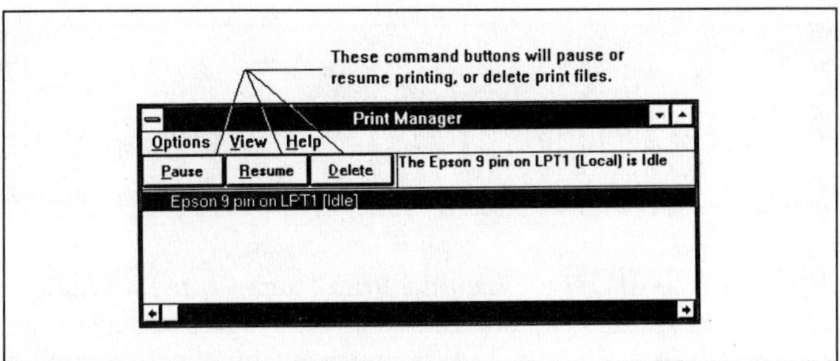

Figure 7.1: The Print Manager screen

with the file name. This can be turned on or off as you choose by selecting Time/Date Sent from the View menu; see "Viewing Time/Date Sent and Print File Size."

RUNNING THE PRINT MANAGER

• EXPLANATION The Print Manager runs automatically whenever you print a file. It shuts down when there are no more files to print. You will rarely need to run the Print Manager by clicking on its icon, as you would most other Windows programs. Windows does allow you to run the Print Manager in this manner, however, because the Print Manager itself may need adjustments. You can configure the Print Manager so that it prints faster, for example, even if there are no files in the queue. (See "Changing the Printing Speed" later in this chapter.)

To Use the Mouse

1. Open the Main program group.
2. Double-click on the Print Manager icon, which is a picture of a laser printer. The Print Manager window will appear.

CHANGING THE PRINTING SPEED

• EXPLANATION When the Print Manager and a Windows application operate simultaneously, some of the computer's processing power is allocated to each program. The Windows application gets more processing power—has a higher priority—than the

Print Manager because the Print Manager operates in the background, sending bits of information to the printer when Windows applications are momentarily idle. If you wish to change this, you can configure the Print Manager so that it has priority equivalent to or higher than any executing Windows applications. This will slow down the applications.

To Use the Mouse

1. Run the Print Manager (see "Running the Print Manager" at the beginning of this chapter), or maximize the Print Manager if it is already running minimized.
2. Pull down the Options menu.
3. Select the default, Medium Priority, if you want the Print Manager and Windows applications to have equal access to Windows' processing power. Select High Priority if you want the Print Manager to have the most processing power. Select Low Priority if you want it to have the least.
4. Close the Print Manager, or minimize it if a file is still printing.

CHANGING PRINT MESSAGES

• **EXPLANATION** The Print Manager is designed to operate in the background, allowing you to continue working while your document prints. The Print Manager will send you messages when, for some reason, you are required to take action. Using the Options menu, you can control what kind of messages the Print Manager displays and when it displays them. There are three ways in which the Print Manager can display messages:

- Alert Always—the Print Manager will interrupt your work session and display a message box requesting user interaction.

- Flash if Inactive—if the Print Manager is minimized or open but inactive, it will cause the computer to beep and then make the Print Manager icon flash, indicating that user interaction is needed.
- Ignore if Inactive—the Print Manager will ignore the condition that requires user interaction unless the Print Manager window is open. Printing will stop.

To Use the Mouse

1. Run the Print Manager (see "Running the Print Manager" at the beginning of this chapter), or maximize the Print Manager.
2. Pull down the Options menu.
3. Select Alert Always, Flash if Inactive, or Ignore if Inactive, according to the criteria listed above.
4. Close the Print Manager or minimize it if a file is still printing.

VIEWING TIME/DATE SENT AND PRINT FILE SIZE

• EXPLANATION When a file is printing, the Print Manager displays the file's name on screen. You can choose to display the time and date the file was sent to the Print Manager and the size of the print file along with the file's name.

To Use the Mouse

1. Run or maximize the Print Manager.
2. Pull down the View menu and select Time/Date Sent or Print File Size.

To Use the Keyboard

1. Run or maximize the Print Manager.
2. Press Alt-V to pull down the View menu.
3. Type **T** to select Time/Date Sent or type **P** to select Print File Size.

Notes Once you select either option, the View menu will close. Pull it down again and you will see a check mark beside the option that you selected, indicating that it is active.

CHANGING THE ORDER OF THE PRINT QUEUE

• **EXPLANATION** When multiple files are passed to the Print Manager, they are placed in the print queue and printed in the order they were received. Using the Print Manager, you can change the order of files in the print queue, and thus change the order in which they are printed.

To Use the Mouse

1. Maximize the Print Manager.
2. Move the mouse pointer onto the Print Manager workspace and over the name of the print file you wish to move, then click on it and hold the mouse button.
3. Drag the file to its new position and release the mouse button.

To Use the Keyboard

1. Maximize the Print Manager.
2. Use the direction keys to select the file you wish to move.

3. Press and hold the Ctrl key.
4. Use the direction keys to move the file to its new position.
5. Release the Ctrl key.

DELETING A FILE FROM THE PRINT QUEUE

• EXPLANATION After you have submitted a print file to the Print Manager, you may change your mind and decide not to print it. To stop the file from printing, you must delete it from the print queue.

To Use the Mouse

1. Maximize the Print Manager.
2. Select the file you wish to delete from the print queue.
3. Click on the Delete command button. A dialog box will appear, asking you to confirm the deletion.
4. Click on OK.

To Use the Keyboard

1. Maximize the Print Manager.
2. Use the direction keys to select the file you wish to delete from the Print Manager workspace.
3. Press Alt-D. A dialog box will appear, asking you to confirm the deletion.
4. Press ↵.

Notes If you delete a file from the queue while it is being printed, you may leave the printer with information still in its buffer. After deleting the file from the queue, turn the printer off and then on again. If you are using a printer with a tractor feed, don't forget to align the top of the new page with the print head.

PAUSING AND RESUMING PRINTING

• **EXPLANATION** There may be times when you want to pause the processing of the print queue so you can examine the files in the queue, move them, or delete them. The Print Manager allows you to pause the queue processing. This means that when the current file finishes printing, the next file in the queue will not automatically start printing. The Print Manager's Pause command does *not* allow you to stop the current print file from printing, unless you are printing on a network that allows such interruptions.

To Use the Mouse

1. Maximize the Print Manager.
2. Select the current printer by clicking on its name.
3. Click on the Pause command button. Queue processing will stop.
4. Click on the Resume command button to resume queue processing.

To Use the Keyboard

1. Maximize the Print Manager.
2. Use the direction keys to select the current printer.
3. Press Alt-P. Queue processing will stop.
4. Press Alt-R to resume queue processing.

VIEWING AN ENTIRE NETWORK QUEUE

• **EXPLANATION** If you are using Windows to print to a network printer, the Print Manager workspace displays only the files *you* have sent to the printer. You can also view the entire network printer queue.

To Use the Mouse

1. Run the Print Manager (see "Running the Print Manager" at the beginning of this chapter), or maximize the Print Manager.
2. Select the network printer by moving the mouse pointer over the information line that describes that printer and clicking on it.
3. Pull down the View menu.
4. Click on Selected Net Queue. A dialog box will appear with the contents of the network printer queue displayed inside it.
5. Click on Close when you are done.

VIEWING OTHER NETWORK QUEUES

• **EXPLANATION** If you are using Windows on a network, you have the option of viewing not only the network queue to which you are connected, but other queues as well.

To Use the Mouse

1. Run the Print Manager (see "Running the Print Manager" at the beginning of this chapter), or maximize the Print Manager.
2. Pull down the View menu and select Other Net Queue. A dialog box will appear, asking you to type the network path name of the print queue you wish to view.
3. Type the network path name in the Network Queue text box.
4. Click on View. The Print Manager will display information on the network queue in a box above the Network Queue dialog box.

UPDATING NETWORK QUEUES

• **EXPLANATION** Network queue information that appears in the Print Manager is updated at regular intervals, which are determined by your network software. You have the option of manually updating the network queue information to determine the current state of the queue.

To Use the Mouse

1. Run the Print Manager (see "Running the Print Manager" at the beginning of this chapter), or maximize the Print Manager.
2. Pull down the View menu and select Update Net Queues. The network queue information will be updated.

Chapter 8

THE MACRO RECORDER

The Windows macro Recorder is a program that records keystrokes and mouse movements and plays them back at a later time. Using Recorder you can make a record, called a *macro*, of any often used mouse movements or key sequences. Then you can play the macro back later with a single keystroke.

Although Recorder will record both mouse movements and keystrokes, it is far preferable to record keystrokes. When tracking mouse movements, Recorder has to track the mouse's coordinates and there are literally thousands of coordinates on the standard video display. In contrast, there are only 101 keys and in any case, recording keystrokes usually involves only a series of key sequences (Alt-F to open the file menu, for example).

Recording macros and making use of them is a tricky proposition. You may record a macro, attempt to play it, and be confronted with one of several types of error messages. This usually means that you need to adjust the macro's properties; see "Changing a Macro's Properties."

RUNNING RECORDER

• **EXPLANATION** Recorder must be run, like other Windows programs. Its icon is located in the Accessories program group.

To Use the Mouse

1. Open the Accessories program group.
2. Double-click on the Recorder icon, which is a picture of a motion picture camera or a video camera (depending on

whether you were a child before or after 1980). The Recorder window will appear.

Notes When you run Recorder for the first time, there won't be any macros, of course, so the workspace will be blank. Later, when you have some macros recorded and saved to disk, you can load them into Recorder and they will appear in the list.

CHANGING THE RECORDER'S OPTIONS

• EXPLANATION Recorder has several options that control how it executes. They are accessed through the Options menu. The Options menu contains four options, the first three of which are toggles. Click on them to switch between active and inactive states. (A check mark appears beside a toggle menu option when it's active.) The fourth option involves a dialog box. The choices on the Options menu are as follows:

- Ctrl-Break Checking—stops Recorder from detecting a Ctrl-Break key sequence, which would normally interrupt macro execution. Use this option to prevent the user from interrupting a macro.
- Shortcut Keys—stops Recorder from detecting shortcut keys. Use this option if an active macro uses a shortcut key that is also used by a currently executing program.
- Minimize on Use—reduces the Recorder to an icon when a macro is played.
- Preferences—invokes the Preferences dialog box, which lets you change the default settings for Recorder. The settings you can adjust are: whether a macro plays only in the application in which it was recorded or in any application; the speed at which the macro replays; the type of mouse movements recorded; and whether a macro is recorded relative to the screen or to a window.

To Use the Mouse

- Pull down the Options menu and select the desired option. If you select a toggle, a check mark will either appear or disappear, depending on whether you toggle on or off. If you select Preferences, the Preferences dialog box will appear. Change one or more default settings, then click on OK.

RECORDING A MACRO

• EXPLANATION At the beginning of the macro recording process, you will assign each macro a name and a shortcut key. The macro name can be up to 40 characters long.

The shortcut key is the key sequence that will invoke the macro you record. A shortcut key can be a single keystroke or a combination of keystrokes. It usually is some combination of Ctrl, Shift, Alt, and any other key.

Although Windows Recorder will allow you to create macros based on the Alt key (Alt-F1, Alt-PgDn, etc.), it probably is not a good idea to do so. Windows has its own set of shortcut keys based on the Alt key (to access pull-down menus, etc.). If you create macros based on it too, they may interfere with Windows' functioning.

To Use the Mouse

1. Run Windows Recorder and then minimize it (see "Running Recorder" at the beginning of this chapter).
2. Run the application in which the macro will operate, and position the cursor at exactly the point where the macro will begin.
3. Restore the Recorder icon to a window.
4. Open the Macro menu and select Record. You will see the screen depicted in Figure 8.1.

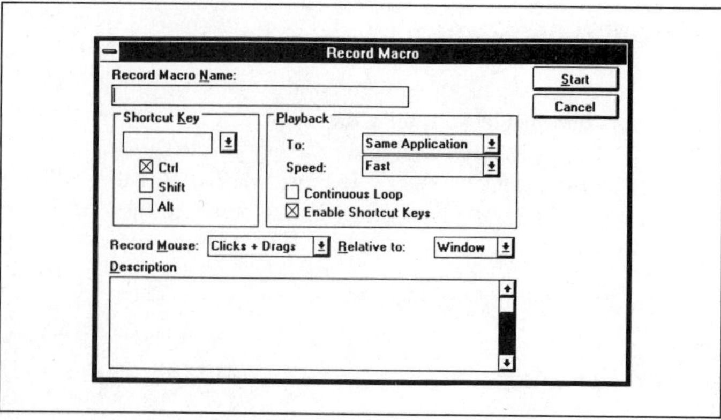

Figure 8.1: The Record Macro dialog box

5. Type a name for the macro in the Record Macro Name text box.
6. Click on the Shift or Alt check boxes to make the macro key begin with the specified keystroke. By default, the Ctrl box is already checked. (Ctrl, Shift, and Alt are not mutually exclusive; you can select any combination of the three.) If a check appears beside the keystroke, that keystroke is part of the shortcut key. If all three keystrokes are checked, the macro begins with the key sequence, Ctrl-Shift-Alt.
7. If you want the macro to end in an alphanumeric key, click on the Shortcut Key box and type the letter or number.
8. If you want the macro to begin with a non-alphanumeric key (PgDn, F1, etc.), click on the arrow on the right side of the Shortcut Key drop-down list box. You will see a list of available keys that can end the shortcut key; select a key.
9. Click on the Start command button. Recorder will become minimized, its icon will start blinking, and the application in which the macro is to execute will become active.
10. Perform the keystrokes and mouse movements you wish to record.

11. When you are done, click on the Recorder. If the application you are in is maximized, press Ctrl-Break. A dialog box will appear, offering you the options of saving the macro, resuming it, or canceling it.
12. Select Save Macro, then click on OK.

RUNNING A MACRO

• **EXPLANATION** To run a macro is to enact a previously recorded series of keystrokes and/or mouse movements. Your keyboard and mouse are temporarily turned off while the macro executes. (You can interrupt the macro by pressing Ctrl-Break.)

To run a macro, Windows Recorder must be active and the desired macro must be loaded into the program. This involves using a macro that was just created, or loading a previously recorded macro from disk (see "Loading a Macro File from Disk").

To Use the Mouse

1. Place the cursor or mouse pointer at the location where you wish the macro to execute.
2. Restore the Recorder icon to a window.
3. If multiple macros appear in the recorder window, select the one you wish to execute.
4. Pull down the Macro menu and select Run. The macro will execute.

To Use the Keyboard

- Place the cursor or mouse pointer at the location where you wish the macro to execute, and press the shortcut key.

CHANGING A MACRO'S PROPERTIES

• EXPLANATION A macro's properties are those features that govern how the macro executes. If you record a macro, attempt to execute it, and get an error message, changing its properties may allow it to execute successfully.

The properties that you can change are: the macro name; its shortcut key assignment; its description; whether the macro plays back only in the application in which it was recorded, or in any Windows program; the speed at which the macro plays back; whether or not the macro plays back continuously; and whether or not the macro can itself contain shortcut keys that invoke other macros. The only setting you cannot change is Mouse Coordinates Relative To.

To Use the Mouse

Start by making sure the Recorder is on screen and that the macro whose properties you wish to change is listed in the Recorder workspace.

1. Select the macro by clicking on its listing in the Recorder workspace.
2. Pull down the Macro menu and select Properties. A screen very similar to the one depicted in Figure 8.1 will appear.
3. Change any of the properties described above.
4. Click on OK.
5. Save the current macro file to make the changes permanent.

SAVING A MACRO FILE

• **EXPLANATION** Macros can be saved to disk and reused at a later time. When you save a macro file, all of the macros currently in memory are written to disk. Before you can save a set of macros, the macros must be recorded and listed in the Recorder workspace. Macro disk files end in a .REC extension.

To Use the Mouse

1. Pull down the file menu and select Save. A dialog box will appear, asking you to key in the name of the macro file.
2. Type the name of the macro file, leaving off the extension.
3. Click on OK.

LOADING A MACRO FILE FROM DISK

• **EXPLANATION** Before you can use any macros that have been saved to disk, you must load the macro file into the Recorder.

To Use the Mouse

1. Run Recorder. (See "Running Recorder" at the beginning of this chapter.)
2. Pull down the file menu and select Open. A dialog box will appear, showing the names of the available macro files.
3. Click on the name of the macro file you wish to load, then click on OK.

Chapter 9

THE PIF EDITOR

PIF is an acronym for *program information file*. A PIF file contains information that Windows uses to run a standard DOS application in a way that is appropriate for that application. A PIF file tells Windows what the program's name is, what kind of video it uses, how much memory it requires, what ports it accesses, and more. (Each non-Windows application should have its own PIF file.)

The PIF Editor is a Windows accessory program that creates, edits, and saves PIF files. If you are running Windows in 386 Enhanced mode, the PIF Editor allows you to adjust the multitasking characteristics of a DOS application. You can specify how much CPU time it uses, how it should access extended memory, and in what way it should handle high-resolution graphics.

The PIF Editor window contains a series of parameters that you can adjust. These parameters differ between Real/Standard modes and 386 Enhanced mode. They are listed below; those that are available only in a certain operating mode are specified.

- Program Filename—the complete path and name of the program file.
- Window Title—the program name you want to appear in the window's title bar.
- Optional Parameters—any alphanumeric character string that follows the Program Filename. An optional parameter might be the name of a document or database with which you want the program to work.
- Start-up Directory—the directory which the DOS application will address when it starts. Some DOS programs need to know where certain files are before they can run. Specify their location with this parameter.
- Video Mode—an option available in Real and Standard modes only. It tells Windows what type of video the application uses so it can allocate the correct amount of video memory.

- Display Usage—a parameter available only in 386 Enhanced mode. It tells Windows to run the application using the full screen, or in a window.
- Memory Requirements—specifies the amount of memory required for the application to run. In 386 Enhanced mode, you can also specify the amount of memory the application would like to have.
- XMS Memory—tells Windows how much extended memory to supply to an application that uses the Lotus-Intel-Microsoft-AST extended memory specification. In 386 Enhanced mode, it is available through the Advanced Options screen.
- Directly Modifies—tells Windows that the application will attempt to communicate directly with the computer's serial ports and/or the keyboard. This parameter is available only in Real and Standard modes.
- Prevent Program Switch—an option that, when active, prevents you from switching back to Windows while the application is executing. This conserves memory. To switch back to Windows, you have to quit the application. Available only in Real and Standard modes.
- No Screen Exchange—allows you to "turn off" Windows' ability to cut and paste between DOS applications and Windows, thus freeing up memory for applications. Available only in Real and Standard modes.
- Reserve Shortcut Keys—allows you to "turn off" certain Windows shortcut keys so that applications can use them (some applications use the same key combinations internally that Windows uses for shortcut keys). This option is available in 386 Enhanced mode, but you have to click on the Advanced command button to get to it.
- Execution—available only in 386 Enhanced mode. This parameter allows you to specify whether or not any applications should run in the background while the current application is in the foreground. The Background option tells Windows to run the current application even when it's minimized. The Exclusive option tells Windows not to run any other applications when this application is

running (even if the Execution option for those applications is set to Background).

- Close Window on Exit—tells Windows whether or not to close a program's window once the program stops running.
- Multitasking Options—available only in 386 Enhanced mode. Allows you to adjust the multitasking characteristics of an application.
- Memory Options—available only in 386 Enhanced mode, except for the XMS memory option. Lets you specify how much EMS (expanded memory specification) or XMS memory to allocate to the application.
- Display Options—available only in 386 Enhanced mode. Specifies the type of video the application uses so Windows can allocate the correct amount of memory, and specifies whether or not Windows should monitor video input and output ports.
- Other Options—lets you change an assortment of settings. Lets you specify whether or not text can be pasted into an application quickly; lets you disable certain Windows shortcut key sequences, such as Alt-Esc, in case they are used by the application; lets you specify a new shortcut key sequence that will switch to the application; and lets you allow Windows to close, or terminate, the program even if it is still active.

RUNNING THE PIF EDITOR

• **EXPLANATION** The PIF Editor is a Windows application whose icon is in the Accessories program group.

To Use the Mouse

1. Open the Accessories program group.

2. Double-click on the PIF Editor icon, which is a picture of a tag with the word "PIF" in it. The PIF Editor window will appear.

Notes If Windows is running in Real or Standard mode, the PIF Editor will look like the one pictured in Figure 9.1; if Windows is running in 386 Enhanced mode, it will look like the one in Figure 9.2.

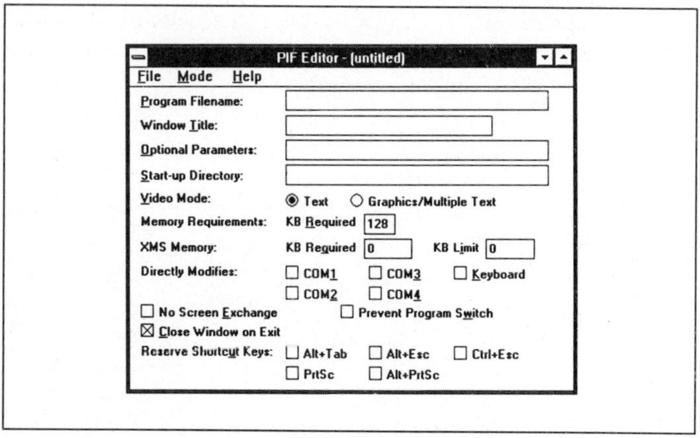

PIF Editor - (untitled)
File Mode Help
Program Filename:
Window Title:
Optional Parameters:
Start-up Directory:
Video Mode: Text Graphics/Multiple Text
Memory Requirements: KB Required 128
XMS Memory: KB Required 0 KB Limit 0
Directly Modifies: COM1 COM3 Keyboard
COM2 COM4
No Screen Exchange Prevent Program Switch
Close Window on Exit
Reserve Shortcut Keys: Alt+Tab Alt+Esc Ctrl+Esc
PrtSc Alt+PrtSc

Figure 9.1: The PIF Editor (Real/Standard mode)

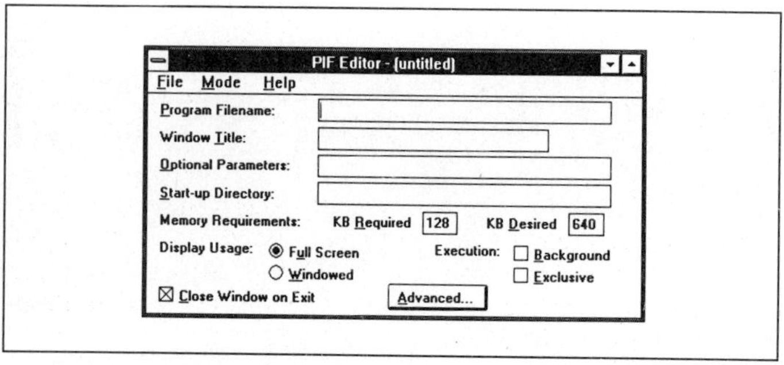

PIF Editor - (untitled)
File Mode Help
Program Filename:
Window Title:
Optional Parameters:
Start-up Directory:
Memory Requirements: KB Required 128 KB Desired 640
Display Usage: Full Screen Execution: Background
Windowed Exclusive
Close Window on Exit Advanced...

Figure 9.2: The PIF Editor (386 Enhanced mode)

OPENING A PIF FILE

• EXPLANATION Windows comes with a PIF file that contains default PIF settings. It is called _DEFAULT.PIF. These default settings are used if the application doesn't have its own PIF file. You may want to open this file and edit it to suit your needs. Also, many standard DOS applications are shipped with a PIF file and you may need to modify them. Lastly, after you have created and saved your own PIF files, you might need to revise them.

To Use the Mouse

1. Run the PIF Editor (see "Running the PIF Editor" at the beginning of this chapter).
2. Pull down the File menu and select Open. A dialog box containing a list of available PIF files will appear.
3. Click on the file you wish to open, then click on OK.

Notes If the PIF file you are opening was generated by an earlier version of Windows, you will see a warning dialog box informing you of this.

EDITING A PIF FILE

• EXPLANATION To create a new PIF file, you must fill in the blank form, entering all the information Windows needs to run the program effectively. This is accomplished using the standard dialog box interface components: option buttons, check boxes, drop-down list boxes, etc.

To Use the Mouse

1. Run the PIF Editor (see "Running the PIF Editor" at the beginning of this chapter).
2. Start by typing the program file name in the first text box.
3. Move to the next option by clicking on it.
4. Edit the parameters as necessary and according to their descriptions at the beginning of this chapter.

To Use the Keyboard

1. Run the PIF Editor (see "Running the PIF Editor" at the beginning of this chapter).
2. Start by typing the program file name in the first text box.
3. Move to the next parameter by pressing the Tab key; move backwards by pressing Shift-Tab.
4. Edit the options as necessary and according to their descriptions at the beginning of this chapter.

SAVING A PIF FILE

• **EXPLANATION** After you have edited a PIF file, you will need to save it.

To Use the Mouse

1. Pull down the File menu and select Save. A dialog box will appear, asking you to type a name for the PIF file. Windows will suggest a file name based upon your entry in the Program Filename option.
2. Accept the suggested file name or edit it to suit you.
3. Click on OK.

Chapter 10

WINDOWS TEXT EDITING

MICROSOFT WRITE

Write is a word processing program from Microsoft that works within the Windows 3.0 environment. Write performs all necessary word processing functions, such as block copying, moving, and deletion. It creates and manipulates italic, superscript, subscript, boldfaced, and underlined text. Write has an undo function, and can find text within a document and replace it with whatever text you designate. Write will import files created by Microsoft WORD, and vice versa. It does not import files from Microsoft Word for Windows, but that product will export its documents to the Write file format.

RUNNING WRITE

• EXPLANATION Write is a Windows application whose icon is in the Accessories program group.

To Use the Mouse

1. Open the Accessories program group.
2. Double-click on the Write icon, which is a picture of a fountain pen inscribing the letter "A." The Write window will appear.

SAVING A WRITE DOCUMENT

• EXPLANATION Write will save any document you edit to a disk file. To save a document, start with the Write window open and the text you wish to save on screen. By default, all Write documents have a .WRI extension.

To Use the Mouse

1. Pull down the File menu and select Save. A dialog box will appear, prompting you to supply the name of the disk file.
2. Type the file name.
3. Click on OK.

To Use the Keyboard

1. Press Alt-F.
2. Type **S**. A dialog box will appear, prompting you to supply the name of the disk file.
3. Type the file name.
4. Press ↵.

Notes If the file being saved already has a name (because you previously saved it), Write will not prompt you for the file name. It will store the file to disk right away.

SAVING A WRITE DOCUMENT IN WORD FORMAT

• EXPLANATION Write will save any document in the Microsoft WORD file format. It will not save documents in the Word for Windows file format.

To Use the Mouse

Start with the Write window open and the text you wish to save on screen.

1. Pull down the File menu. If you haven't saved the text before, select Save. If you have saved the text before, select Save As. A dialog box will appear, prompting you to supply the name of the disk file.

2. Type the file name without the extension.
3. Click on the Microsoft WORD File Format check box.
4. Click on OK.

Notes When Write saves a document to the Microsoft WORD format, it automatically assigns the file a .DOC extension.

OPENING A WRITE DOCUMENT

• EXPLANATION To open a document is to read it from disk into Write. This is accomplished using the File menu.

To Use the Mouse

Start with the Write window on screen.

1. Pull down the File menu and select Open. A dialog box will appear, listing the available files. This displays, by default, Write files in the current directory. Files in other directories can be accessed and listed by clicking on entries in the Directories list box.
2. Click on the file you wish to open, then click on OK.

PRINTING A DOCUMENT

• EXPLANATION Printing a document from Write is a very simple procedure.

To Use the Mouse

1. Pull down the File menu and select Print. You will see the Print dialog box.
2. Configure the settings within the dialog box to suit your needs. You can specify the number of copies, the range of pages to print, and—with some printers—whether or not to print in draft quality.
3. Click on OK.

CHANGING PRINTERS

• EXPLANATION Write gives you the option of printing to a printer other than the default printer.

To Use the Mouse

1. Pull down the File menu and select Printer Setup. A Printer Setup dialog box will appear.
2. Click on the name of the printer to which you wish to switch.
3. Click on OK.

DISPLAYING AND HIDING THE RULER

• EXPLANATION The Ruler is a graphic image of a ruler that Write places at the top of the window. The Ruler helps you understand exactly where text is placed on the page. In addition, it lets you easily set tabs, indents, line spacing, and justification. There is one procedure for both displaying and hiding the Ruler; it toggles the Ruler on and off. To display the Ruler, start with the Write window on screen.

To Use the Mouse

- Pull down the Document menu and select Ruler On.

To Use the Keyboard

1. Press Alt-D.
2. Type **R**.

SETTING TABS

• EXPLANATION Write's tabs are preset at one-half inch. You can override these tabs and set up to 12 tabs of your own. You can set either regular or decimal tabs. (A decimal tab is one in which numbers that are typed align on their decimal points.)

To Use the Mouse

1. Pull down the Document window and select Tabs. The Tabs dialog box, pictured in Figure 10.1, will appear. The text boxes labeled *Positions* are where you key in the tab position. The text box for the first tab is the upper left one; they run from left to right, then move down to the second *Positions* line.

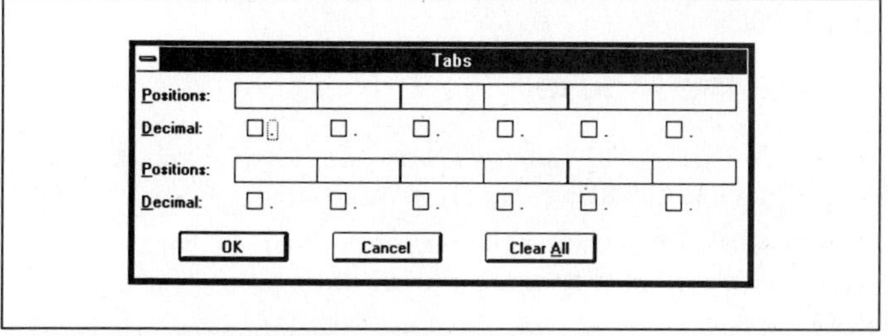

Figure 10.1: The Tabs dialog box

2. Click on the box corresponding to the tab you wish to set.
3. Type a position. The position will represent the distance of the tab from the left margin, in inches.
4. Click on the decimal check box below the Position text box if you are creating a decimal tab.
5. Repeat steps 2, 3, and 4 as needed.
6. Click on OK.

SETTING TABS WITH THE RULER

• EXPLANATION Write offers an easy and intuitive way to set tabs, using the Ruler. The Ruler uses tab icons and tab markers to help you create tabs and to indicate their location; see Figure 10.2.

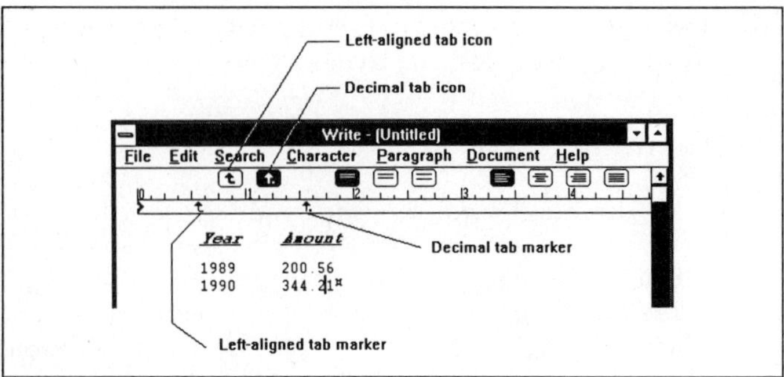

Figure 10.2: The Ruler, with tab components

To Use the Mouse

1. Make sure the Ruler is visible (see "Displaying and Hiding the Ruler" earlier in this chapter).
2. Click either the left-aligned or decimal tab icon to tell Write what type of tab you are setting.
3. Place the mouse pointer over the point on the ruler line where you want the tab, and click. A tab marker will appear. Be careful not to click on the Ruler's graduations, as this won't produce the desired effect. Instead, click in the empty line below the graduation.

Notes To delete tabs, pull down the Document menu and select Tabs. When the Tabs dialog box appears, select the position box for the tab you wish to delete, and remove the measurement. If you want to delete all the tabs, click on the Clear All command button.

SETTING MARGINS

• EXPLANATION Margins are the boundaries of the printed page. The left and right margins are the distances between the text and the left and right sides of the page, respectively. The top margin is the distance between the first line of text and the top of the page, and the bottom margin is the distance between the baseline of the text and the bottom of the page. Write allows you to change all of these margins.

Write uses inches as its default measurement. If you wish to change this to centimeters, click on the Cm option button at the bottom of the Page Layout screen, described below.

To Use the Mouse

1. Pull down the Document menu and select Page Layout. A dialog box containing text boxes for the left, right, top, and bottom margins will appear.
2. Move the mouse pointer over the text box for the margin you wish to change, and click.
3. Type the new margin measurement.
4. Click on OK.

SELECTING TEXT

• **EXPLANATION** When working with Write, you can select portions of text and then modify that text. You can change its font style, for example, or underline or boldface it. You can also cut the text into the Clipboard and copy it to another place in the document, or into a different application.

To Use the Mouse

Start with the text you wish to select visible in the Write window.

1. Place the mouse pointer on the upper-left corner of the text you wish to select.
2. Click and hold down the left mouse button.
3. Drag the pointer to the lower right corner of the text.
4. Release the mouse button. The text is now selected.

See Also Changing the Text Style, Changing Fonts and Font Sizes, Cutting/Copying and Pasting Text

SELECTING TEXT USING THE SELECTION AREA

• EXPLANATION Write offers an additional method for selecting text using a portion of the screen called the *selection area*. The selection area is an invisible vertical line on the left side of the Write workspace; the pointer slants to the right when it is over the selection area.

The following list describes procedures for selecting text using the various selection area options.

- **A single line**. From the selection area, point to the line and click the mouse.
- **Multiple lines**. From the selection area, point to the line, click and hold down the mouse button, then drag the pointer up or down.
- **A paragraph**. From the selection area, point to the paragraph and double-click.
- **Multiple paragraphs**. From the selection area, point to the paragraph, double-click and hold down the mouse button, then drag the pointer up or down.
- **A text range**. Select the beginning paragraph or line. Move the pointer to the selection area adjacent to the ending paragraph or line. Hold down the Shift key and click the mouse button.
- **The whole document**. Place the pointer in the selection area, hold down the Ctrl key, and click left.

CHANGING FONTS AND FONT SIZES

• EXPLANATION A font is a graphically rendered image of a particular typeface. Fonts are named after the typefaces they represent—Courier, Times Roman, Helvetica, etc. The default font for Write is Courier, set at 10 characters per inch (CPI). You can change fonts at any time and use any of the fonts installed in the Windows environment.

To Use the Mouse

1. Place the cursor at the location where you want to start typing in the new font.
2. Pull down the Character menu and select Fonts. A dialog box with a list box containing the available fonts will appear. If a font is available in multiple point sizes, an additional list box showing the sizes will appear.
3. Scroll through the Fonts list box until you see the font you want.
4. Click on the font name. Click also on the font point size in the Sizes list box, if that is available.
5. Click on OK.

Notes To change the font of already selected text, follow the procedure described in "Selecting Text" earlier in this chapter. Then follow steps 2 through 5 listed above.

CHANGING THE TEXT STYLE

• EXPLANATION The term "text style" refers to the appearance of text both on screen and on the printed page. Write will format text in several styles: underlined, boldfaced, italic, superscript, and subscript.

To Use the Mouse

1. Place the cursor at the location where you want to start typing in the new style.
2. Pull down the Character menu and select the desired style.

Notes To change the style of already selected text, follow the procedure described in "Selecting Text" earlier in this chapter. Then follow step 2 listed above.

CUTTING/COPYING AND PASTING TEXT

• EXPLANATION Like almost every other Windows program, Write will allow you to select information and copy it into a reserved portion of memory called the Clipboard. You can delete the selected text as you place it in the Clipboard, which is called *cutting,* or you can simply copy it. Text placed in the Clipboard can be copied back into the current document at any point you specify. This is called *pasting*. The text can also be pasted into any other application running under Windows that will accept textual data.

To Use the Mouse

1. Place the mouse pointer on the upper-left corner of the text you wish to select.
2. Click and hold down the left mouse button.
3. Drag the pointer to the lower-right corner of the text.
4. Release the mouse button. The text is now selected.
5. Pull down the Edit menu and select either Cut or Copy. The selected text is now in the Clipboard. You can go on from here and paste the text somewhere else in the current document, or leave Write and paste the text into another application.
6. Place the cursor at exactly the point where you want the pasted text to appear.
7. Pull down the Edit menu and select Paste. The text in the Clipboard will be placed at the specified point.

See Also Pasting Data from the Clipboard (Ch. 4)

FINDING TEXT

• EXPLANATION Write has the ability to search for and find any characters you specify.

To Use the Mouse

1. Pull down the Search menu and select Find. A dialog box will appear, with a text box and two check boxes inside.
2. Key in the text for which you wish to search.
3. If you want to search for the specified text as a whole word, click on the Whole Word check box. If you don't click on this check box, Write will find every occurrence of the specified text, no matter what its context. If you were searching for the word "go," for example, Write would find "gone," and "gooney."
4. If you want Write to search for *exactly* the text you typed, including matching upper- and lowercase letters, then click on the Match Upper/Lowercase check box.
5. Click on the Find Next command button. Write will find the first occurrence of the search target in the text.
6. If you wish to find the next occurrence of the same text, press F3, the Repeat Last Find key. You can also select Repeat Last Find from the Search menu.

FINDING AND CHANGING A BLOCK OF TEXT

• **EXPLANATION** Write will search for any characters you specify and replace them with any other characters.

To Use the Mouse

1. Pull down the Search menu and select Change. A dialog box will appear, with two text boxes and two check boxes inside it.
2. Key the text for which you wish to search into the Find What text box. To search for the specified text as a whole word, click on the Whole Word check box before you click on the Find Next command button. (If you don't click on

the Whole Word check box, Write will find every occurrence of the specified text, no matter what its context. If you were searching for the word "go," for example, Write would find "gone," and "gooney.") If you want Write to search for *exactly* the text you type, including matching upper- and lowercase letters, then click on the Match Upper/Lowercase check box.

3. Click on the Change To text box, then type the text you wish to change to.
4. If you click on the Find Next command button, Write will find the first occurrence of the search target.
5. Click on Change, then Find. Write will replace the search target with the specified text, and then move on to the next occurrence of the target.
6. Repeat step 5 as necessary. If you wish, you can change all occurrences of the target by clicking on the Change All command button.

INSERTING A PICTURE

• EXPLANATION You can insert pictures from other programs into Write documents. This is accomplished using the Clipboard. When a picture is inserted into Write, it is automatically lined up on the left side of the screen. It is also presented at a resolution that matches the default printer, not the video display.

To Use the Mouse

Start with Write as a minimized icon on the Windows desktop, and the application that is the source of the picture in an open window on screen.

1. Cut the desired picture into the Windows Clipboard (see "Cutting or Copying Data into the Clipboard" in Chapter 4).
2. Maximize or restore Write.
3. Place the mouse pointer at the location where you want the picture to appear.

4. Pull down the Edit menu and select Paste. The picture will appear in the Write workspace.

SIZING A PICTURE

• EXPLANATION Write allows you to adjust the size of a picture so that you can create correctly formatted documents. When you size a picture, the upper-left corner of the image stays "anchored" in its original position. Using the mouse, you adjust the placement of the lower-right corner of the image and thus control its size.

To Use the Mouse

1. Click on the picture to select it. The picture will appear in inverse colors.
2. Pull down the Edit menu and select Size Picture. The mouse pointer will change into a picture of a box. As you move the box around on screen, you will see a vertical line and a left-pointing horizontal line stemming from it.
3. Move the box-pointer to the location where you want the lower-right corner to be.
4. Click the left mouse button.

MOVING A PICTURE

• EXPLANATION Write allows you to move a picture horizontally on screen.

To Use the Mouse

1. Click on the picture to select it. The picture will appear in inverse colors.
2. Pull down the Edit menu and select Move Picture. The mouse pointer will change into a picture of a box. A rectangle that is exactly the shape of the selected picture will surround it.

3. Move the box-pointer and the rectangle to the desired location.
4. Click the left mouse button.

NOTEPAD

Windows Notepad is an ASCII (American Standard Code for Information Interchange) text editor. Notepad is useful for writing quick notes and memos, and editing any other type of ASCII file. You can use Notepad to create and edit batch files, or to edit the system configuration files, CONFIG.SYS and AUTOEXEC.BAT. Notepad offers only rudimentary word processing features, such as word wrap and the ability to search for any text you specify. It does not format text or render it boldfaced, underlined, or italic.

RUNNING NOTEPAD AND CREATING A NOTE

• **EXPLANATION** Notepad is a Windows application whose icon is in the Accessories program group.

To Use the Mouse

1. Open the Accessories program group.
2. Double-click on the Notepad icon, which is a picture of a partially open spiral-bound notepad. The Notepad window will appear.
3. To create a note, start typing. When you reach the right side of the window, the text will disappear off the edge as you type. To make the text automatically move to the next line, set Notepad's word wrap feature on. See "Setting Word Wrap" later in this chapter.

SAVING A NOTE

• EXPLANATION When Notepad saves a file, it saves the text in standard ASCII format. It also writes the file to the Windows directory, unless you specify otherwise when you save it.

To Use the Mouse

1. Pull down the File menu and select Save. A dialog box will appear, prompting you for the name of the file.
2. Type in the name of the file. If you leave off a file extension when you type the file name, Notepad will automatically assign the file a .TXT extension. If you specify a different extension, Notepad will use it.

OPENING A NOTE

• EXPLANATION To open a file is to read it from disk into Notepad, and make it available for editing.

To Use the Mouse

1. Pull down the File menu and select Open. The File Open dialog box will appear, listing all available files and prompting you for a file name. The files listed will have .TXT extensions by default. To see a list of different files, press Backspace to erase the file specification in the File Open dialog box. Then type the wildcard file specification for the files you wish to view (***.BAT**, ***.SYS**, etc.), then press ↵.
2. Type the name of the file you wish to open and click on OK, or double-click on the file's name in the list box. The text contained in the specified file will appear in the Notepad workspace.

SETTING WORD WRAP

• EXPLANATION Word wrap is a term that describes a text editor's ability to perceive that the text being typed is about to exceed the right margin, and to automatically place any subsequent text on the next line. In Notepad, you can toggle this feature on or off.

To Use the Mouse

- Pull down the Edit menu and select Word Wrap. A check mark will appear beside the Word Wrap menu option and the Edit menu will retract. The Word Wrap option has just been toggled on.

PRINTING A DOCUMENT

• EXPLANATION Printing a document from Notepad is a very simple procedure. Once you've selected the Print option, Notepad will immediately send the entire document to the printer. You will not be given the option of printing specific pages, as you would be with more powerful text editors.

To Use the Mouse

- Pull down the File menu and select Print.

To Use the Keyboard

- Press Alt-F to pull down the File menu, then type **P** to select the Print option.

CHANGING THE PRINTER

• EXPLANATION Like Write, Notepad gives you the option of printing to a printer other than the default printer.

To Use the Mouse

1. Pull down the File menu and select Printer Setup. A Printer Setup dialog box will appear.
2. Click on the name of the printer to which you wish to switch.
3. Click on OK.

CREATING A DATE LOG

• **EXPLANATION** A date log is a record of the times and dates when a Notepad file was edited. Notepad will keep a date log within a file, provided you specify it as a date log file.

To Use the Mouse

1. Open or create a note (see "Running Notepad and Creating a Note" or "Opening a Note" in this chapter).
2. At the beginning of the first line in the file, type **.LOG**. Make sure you use uppercase letters.
3. Save the note to disk (see "Saving a Note" in this chapter). Now, every time you open this file, Notepad will automatically insert the date at the end of the file.

SELECTING, CUTTING, AND COPYING TEXT

• **EXPLANATION** Text within Notepad can be selected and cut or copied into the Windows Clipboard, much like text in any other Windows program.

To Select Text with the Mouse

Start with the text you wish to select visible in the Notepad workspace.

1. Move the mouse pointer to the beginning of the text. The pointer will change into a vertical bar when it's over the Notepad workspace.

2. Click and hold the mouse button, then move the pointer over the text you wish to select. The selected text will appear in reverse video.
3. Release the left mouse button.

To Cut Selected Text with the Mouse

- Pull down the File menu and select Cut. The selected text will be copied to the Clipboard and deleted from the Notepad workspace.

To Copy Selected Text with the Mouse

- Pull down the File menu and select Copy. The selected text will be copied to the Clipboard and will remain in the Notepad workspace.

FINDING TEXT

• EXPLANATION Notepad can search text and find any string of characters you specify.

To Use the Mouse

1. Pull down the Search menu and select Find. The Find dialog box will appear, prompting you to specify the text for which Notepad will search.
2. Type the text for which you wish to search.
3. Click on the Match Upper/Lowercase check box if you want Notepad to search for *exactly* the text you typed. Click on the Backward option button if you want it to search backward from the current location to the top of the current text file.
4. Click on OK. Notepad will search for and find any occurrence of the specified text. It will search from the current cursor location forward, unless you specified otherwise.
5. To find the next occurrence of the text, pull down the Search menu and select Find Next, or press F3.

INSERTING THE DATE

• EXPLANATION At any point when you are editing a text file, Notepad can insert the date.

To Use the Mouse

1. Place the cursor at exactly the point where you want the date to appear.
2. Pull down the Edit menu and select Time/Date (this feature doesn't work properly yet—you can only insert the date), or press F5.

Chapter 11

PAINTBRUSH

Paintbrush is a drawing program for use with Windows 3.0. Using Paintbrush, you can create, save, modify, and print graphic images. Paintbrush generates detailed color or black-and-white images. Paintbrush has ten basic shapes that the reader may manipulate. These shapes can be modified or stretched, and filled with colors or black-and-white cross-hatching.

Images generated by Paintbrush can be used in any other Windows program that supports bit-mapped graphics, including Windows Write. Windows can use graphics generated by Paintbrush as wallpaper images for the Windows desktop (see "Changing the Desktop Wallpaper" in Chapter 6).

The Paintbrush screen is divided into four areas—the Toolbox, the Linesize Box, the Palette, and the Drawing Area (see Figure 11.1):

- The Toolbox—this area contains symbols, or tools, which indicate what type of drawing action the cursor will perform. Click on the straight line and the cursor will draw straight lines; click on the filled circle and the cursor will draw filled circles. Tools are also available for cutting and pasting, entering text, and erasing.
- The Linesize box—this lets you set the thickness of the lines drawn by Paintbrush. This setting affects the lines in all Paintbrush shapes, not just straight lines. It also affects the eraser and spray can tool size.
- The Palette—this area contains a grid showing the various colors you can select and use.
- The Drawing Area—this is where you create your Paintbrush drawings.

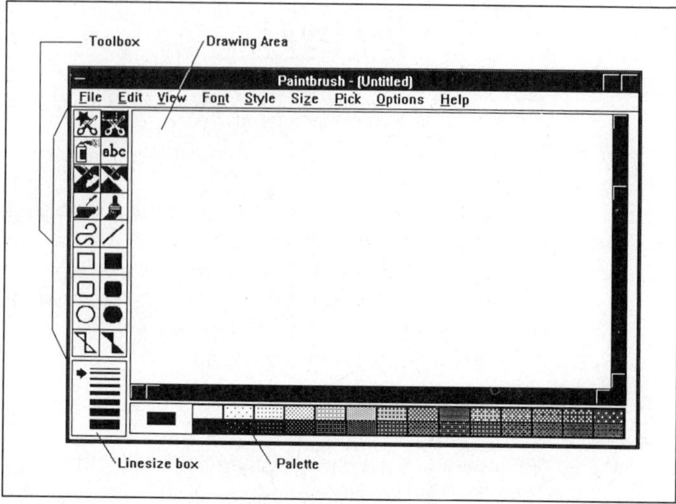

Figure 11.1: The Paintbrush screen

RUNNING PAINTBRUSH

• **EXPLANATION** Paintbrush is a Windows application whose icon is in the Accessories program group.

To Use the Mouse

1. Open the Accessories program group.
2. Double-click on the Paintbrush icon, which is a picture of a painter's palette. The Paintbrush window will appear.

SELECTING A PAINTBRUSH TOOL

• EXPLANATION Before you can use a Paintbrush tool, you must select it. When a tool is selected, its symbol appears in reverse colors (what was white becomes black, and colors switch to alternate colors on the palette). Also, depending on the tool, the size and shape of the cursor change.

To Use the Mouse

- Move the mouse pointer over the desired tool and click.

CREATING A BOX OR CIRCLE

• EXPLANATION Paintbrush lets you create many different types of shapes—circles, squares, and polygons, to name a few. The eight basic shapes in the Paintbrush Toolbox are the box and the filled box; the rounded box and the filled rounded box; the circle/ellipse and the filled circle/ellipse; and the polygon and the filled polygon. See Figure 11.2.

The method for creating all types of boxes and circles is described below. Creating polygons is described in "Creating a Polygon" in this chapter.

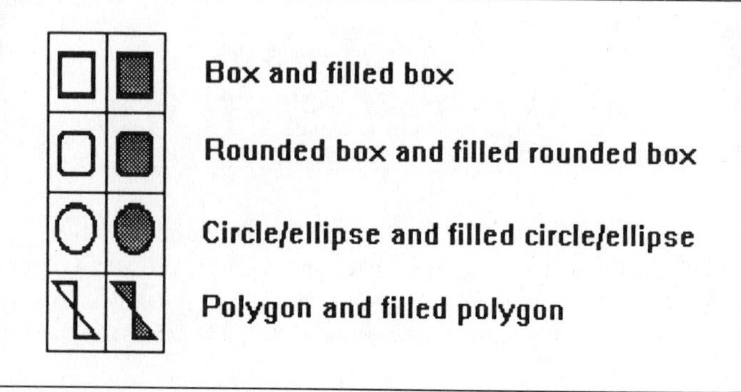

Figure 11.2: The Paintbrush shapes

To Use the Mouse

1. Place the mouse pointer over the shape you wish to create in the Toolbox, and click.
2. Move the pointer out into the drawing area (the pointer will change into a cross), and place it at the location where you want the upper-left corner of your shape to begin.
3. Click and hold the left mouse button.
4. Drag the pointer to the location where you want the lower-right corner of the shape to be.
5. Release the left mouse button.

Notes You can control the appearance of shapes a great deal by setting the line size. See "Setting the Line Size" later in this chapter.

CREATING A POLYGON

• EXPLANATION Creating a polygon is slightly different from creating other shapes. You first create one side of the polygon, then the others in sequence.

To Use the Mouse

1. Place the mouse pointer over the polygon tool in the Toolbox, and click.
2. Move the pointer out into the drawing area (the pointer will change into a cross), and place it at the location where you want the line that will make up the first side of the polygon to begin.
3. Click and hold the left mouse button.
4. Drag the pointer to the location where you want the line to end. Release the left mouse button.
5. Repeat steps 3 and 4 until the next-to-last side has been defined. Do not define the last line in the polygon.
6. Double-click the left mouse button. A line will appear between the end of the last line drawn and the starting point of the first line, completing the polygon.

CHANGING THE FILL WITH THE PAINT ROLLER

• **EXPLANATION** The paint roller is a Paintbrush tool that will fill any enclosed shape with any color or cross-hatch pattern. If used in a non-enclosed space, it will fill the entire drawing area with the new color or pattern.

To Use the Mouse

Start with a shape on the screen to hold the fill color or pattern. See "Creating a Box or Circle" or "Creating a Polygon" in this chapter.

1. Move the pointer over the palette and click the left mouse button on the color you wish the fill to be. If you are working in black-and-white mode, the palette contains different types of cross-hatching instead of colors; click left on the pattern you choose.

2. Select the paint roller tool by moving the mouse pointer over it and clicking. Once you move the pointer from the Toolbox to the drawing area, the pointer will change into a picture of a paint roller.
3. Place the pointed tip of the paint roller-pointer in the area that you wish to fill, and click left. The area will fill with the specified color or pattern.

USING THE ERASER

• **EXPLANATION** The eraser tool allows you to wipe out any portions of the current drawing contacted by the eraser. It is easy to confuse the eraser with the color eraser; the eraser is the tool in the right-hand column. See Figure 11.3.

To Use the Mouse

1. Select the eraser tool by clicking on it.
2. Move the pointer into the drawing area. It will change into a box, the size of which is determined by the line size setting.
3. Place the box-pointer over the image you wish to erase, then click and hold the left mouse button. The image directly under the box-pointer will be erased.
4. Move the box-pointer around to erase more of the image.
5. Release the mouse button.

Figure 11.3: The eraser tool

SETTING THE LINE SIZE

• EXPLANATION Paintbrush will draw lines in varying degrees of thickness. The line size setting affects the eraser and spray can size—the smaller the line size, the smaller the eraser and spray area. You specify line thickness using the Linesize Box.

To Use the Mouse

1. Move the mouse pointer over the Linesize Box. The pointer will become an arrow positioned on the right side of the Linesize Box.
2. Move the arrow up or down until it is beside the line size you want, then click left.

CREATING A CUTOUT

• EXPLANATION A cutout is a portion of a Paintbrush image, defined by the user, which can be deleted, moved, copied, or sized. There are two cutout tools, a rectangular and a free-form tool, pictured in Figure 11.4.

The rectangular cutout tool allows you to define a rectangular section of the image as the cutout; the free-form tool allows you to

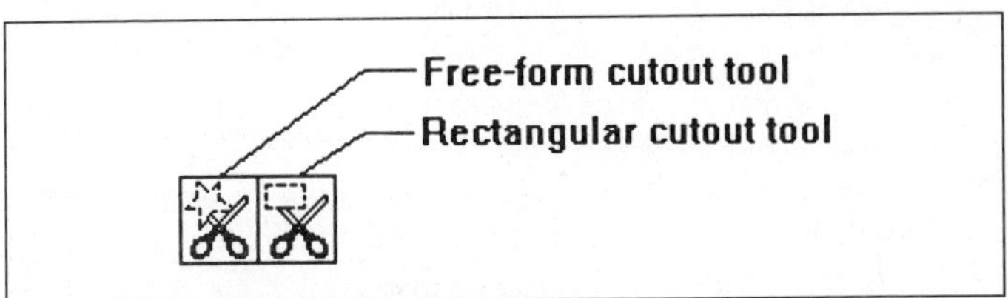

Figure 11.4: The cutout tools

define a section of any shape as the cutout (though you have to have a steady hand to use it for detailed work).

Once you have selected a cutout, you can use the Cut or Copy option in the Edit menu to place it in the Windows Clipboard, where it can be pasted into other Windows applications or back into Paintbrush.

To Use the Rectangular Cutout Tool with the Mouse

1. Move the mouse pointer over the Toolbox and click on the rectangular cutout tool.
2. Place the mouse pointer at the upper-left corner of the rectangular area you wish to select.
3. Click and hold the left mouse button, then drag the pointer to the lower right corner of the area. The outline of a rectangle will appear and move with the pointer.
4. Release the mouse button. The selected area will become a cutout.

To Use the Free-Form Cutout Tool with the Mouse

1. Move the mouse pointer over the Toolbox and click on the free-form cutout tool.
2. Place the mouse pointer at any point around the area you wish to select.
3. Click and hold the left mouse button, then drag the pointer carefully around the area you wish to select. A line that indicates the area selected will follow the pointer as it moves around the image.
4. When you reach the point where you started, release the mouse button. The selected area will become a cutout. You don't have to move the pointer all the way around to where you started. If you release the button before that point, however, Paintbrush will draw a straight line

between the beginning and end points of the line you just defined, possibly intersecting the image you wish to select.

MOVING A CUTOUT

• EXPLANATION By moving a cutout, you can position the image in the cutout anywhere in the Paintbrush workspace that you like.

To Use the Mouse

1. Move the mouse pointer over the selected cutout, then click and hold the left mouse button.
2. Move the cutout anywhere in the Paintbrush workspace.
3. Release the mouse button.

COPYING A CUTOUT

• EXPLANATION By copying a cutout, you can position a copy of the image in the cutout anywhere in the Paintbrush workspace that you like.

To Use the Mouse

1. Move the mouse pointer over the selected cutout, press and hold the Shift key, then click and hold the left mouse button.
2. Move the cutout anywhere in the Paintbrush workspace.
3. Release the Shift key and the mouse button.

DELETING A CUTOUT

• EXPLANATION To delete a cutout, you must first define it (see "Creating a Cutout" in this chapter), then cut it into the Clipboard. (If you like, you can select Copy instead of Cut, and the cutout will remain in the Paintbrush workspace while still being copied into the Clipboard.)

To Use the Mouse

- With the cutout created, pull down the Edit menu and select Cut. The cutout will disappear from the Paintbrush workspace. A copy of it will be placed in the Windows Clipboard.

ZOOMING IN AND OUT

• EXPLANATION By default, Paintbrush allows you to generate an image 8 inches wide by 5 inches high. The opening Paintbrush screen displays only about 40 percent of that area. However, Paintbrush allows you to view the entire drawing area using Zoom Out, so that you can view an entire picture or paste a graphic that is larger than the current screen size. Paintbrush also lets you edit images with very fine precision, using Zoom In. Zoom In will magnify a portion of the Paintbrush screen and let you edit individual pixels.

To Zoom Out Using the Mouse

When a Paintbrush image is zoomed out, only the Edit, View, and Help menus are available.

1. Pull down the View menu and select Zoom Out. The Paintbrush workspace will be redrawn to display the entire image area.
2. To cancel Zoom Out, pull down the View menu and select Zoom In.

Pasting You can paste images into Paintbrush that are larger than the standard Paintbrush workspace by selecting Zoom Out mode first, and then pasting the image. The procedure is slightly different from the standard pasting procedure used in most Windows programs.

1. Make sure Paintbrush is not in Zoom In mode.
2. Cut or copy the image you wish to paste into the Clipboard (see "Creating a Cutout" earlier in this chapter).
3. Pull down the View menu and select Zoom Out. The Paintbrush workspace will redraw to show the entire image area.
4. Pull down the Edit menu and select Paste. A cross-hatched rectangle that represents the image to be pasted will appear.
5. Place the pointer inside the rectangle, click and hold the left mouse button, then move the rectangle to the place where you want the image to appear. Release the mouse button.
6. Move the pointer outside the rectangle and click. If the rectangle takes up the entire image area, move the pointer outside that area and click.

To Zoom In Using the Mouse

1. Pull down the View menu and select Zoom In. The pointer will change into a rectangle that will mark the area to be magnified.
2. Move the rectangle and cover the area you want magnified, then click the left mouse button. Click the left mouse button to change a pixel to the current foreground color; click the right mouse button to change a pixel to the current background color. To change an entire group of

pixels, click and hold the appropriate button, then move the pointer over the pixels you wish to change.

3. To cancel Zoom In, pull down the View menu and select Zoom Out.

PRINTING FROM PAINTBRUSH

• EXPLANATION Paintbrush gives you the ability to print an image in draft (low-resolution) or proof (high-resolution) mode. It also lets you print all or part of an image, and generate single or multiple copies.

To Use the Mouse

1. Pull down the File menu and select Print. The Print dialog box will appear, as shown in Figure 11.5.
2. Set the various print options to suit your needs. Select the Partial option button to print only a portion of the image. Select Use Printer Resolution to print the image at the printer's resolution rather than the screen's. On dot-matrix printers, this results in a printed image that is stretched but of a higher resolution.

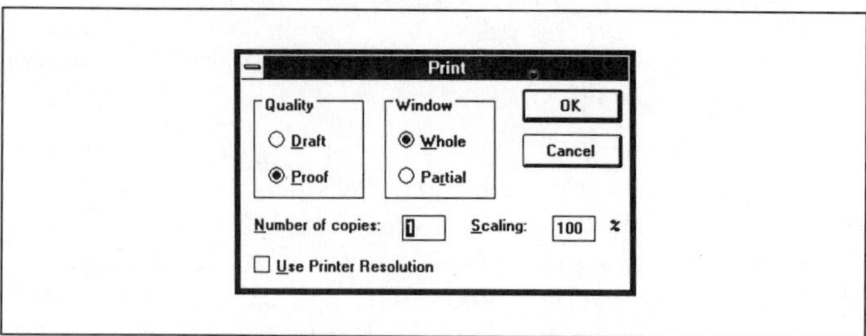

Figure 11.5: The Print dialog box

3. Click on OK. If you chose to print the whole image, Paintbrush will print the image. If you chose to print only a part of the image, the Paintbrush workspace will be redrawn to display the entire image and the pointer will become a cross. Follow steps 4 and 5 only if you chose to print only part of an image.
4. Move the pointer over to the upper-left corner of the area you wish to print, then click and hold the left mouse button.
5. Drag the pointer to the lower-right corner of the area, and release the mouse button. Paintbrush will print the selected image.

Chapter 12

COMMUNICATIONS WITH WINDOWS TERMINAL

Terminal is a Windows application that allows you to connect your computer to another computer and exchange information. Using a computer peripheral called a modem, which connects to your serial port and then to the telephone system, Terminal can access information services like CompuServe or MCI Mail.

The following instructions assume that you are familiar with basic telecommunications concepts.

RUNNING TERMINAL

• **EXPLANATION** Terminal is a Windows application whose icon is in the Accessories program group.

To Use the Mouse

1. Open the Accessories program group.
2. Double-click on the Terminal icon, which is a picture of a telephone with a computer behind it. The Terminal window will appear.

SAVING AND OPENING THE SETTINGS FILE

• **EXPLANATION** Terminal's settings are all the options that are available under the Settings menu:

- Phone Number—lets you specify the telephone number of the host system you are calling.
- Terminal Emulation—sets the type of terminal that Terminal should emulate for this session. See "Changing Terminal Emulation."
- Terminal Preferences—allows you to change the specific characteristics of the current terminal emulation. See "Changing Terminal Settings."
- Text Transfers—lets you change the way in which text is sent and received by Terminal.
- Binary Transfers—specifies the binary transfer protocol to use for this session. See "Setting a Binary Transfer Protocol."
- Communications—lets you change the communications parameters, such as baud rate, data bits, and parity, for the current session. See "Changing Communications Parameters."
- Modem Commands—lets you change the commands Terminal transmits to the modem, such as the dialing prefix and the command to make the modem answer an incoming call.
- Printer Echo—causes incoming text to be sent to the printer. If Local Echo is turned on (see "Changing Terminal Settings"), keystrokes are also sent to the printer.

- Timer Mode—starts a timer running in the lower-right corner of the screen. This is useful for timing costly online sessions. The function keypad must be displayed (see below) for the timer to be displayed.
- Show Function Keys—displays the function keys and their assignments in two rows at the bottom of the screen. Also displays a digital clock that can be used as a timer.

Terminal allows you to save all these settings in a file, so you can load the file and use them again the next time you call the same remote computer.

Terminal is an under-powered version of the DynaComm telecommunications program from FutureSoft Engineering, Inc. Because of this, you can use Terminal settings (TRM) files as DynaComm settings (DCS) files. Just rename the .TRM file with a .DCS extension. This works with Windows Terminal 3.0 and version 3.0 of DynaComm, but may not work with future versions of these programs.

To Save a Settings File Using the Mouse

Start by adjusting all the settings to meet your needs.

1. Pull down the File menu and select Save. If you already have a settings file open, Terminal will save the current settings to that file, and you don't need to perform steps 2 and 3. If you are saving the current settings for the first time, a dialog box will appear, prompting you to key in the name of the settings file.
2. Type the name of the file, without the file extension. When you save the file, Terminal will automatically give the file a .TRM extension.
3. Click on OK.

To Open a Settings File Using the Mouse

1. Pull down the File menu and select Open. A dialog box will appear, with a list of the available settings files in it.

2. Double-click on the name of the file you wish to load.

DISPLAYING THE FUNCTION KEYS

• **EXPLANATION** Function keys F1 through F8 can each have commands assigned to them. The keys are given names and can appear as buttons at the bottom of the Terminal screen. In its default state, Terminal does not display the function key buttons (see Figure 12.1); changing this default is simple.

To Use the Mouse

- Pull down the Settings menu and select Show Function Keys. The bottom of the screen will display the function key buttons.

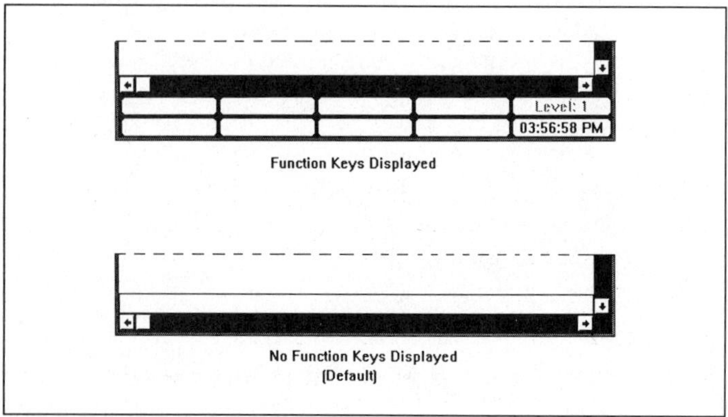

Figure 12.1: Terminal windows with and without function key buttons displayed

ASSIGNING COMMANDS TO FUNCTION KEYS

• **EXPLANATION** Each of the first eight function keys (F1 through F8) can have up to 41 characters assigned to it. The function keys are given names, and can be displayed as buttons at the bottom of the screen. There are four sets, or levels, of function keys available, resulting in a total of 32 possible key assignments. You assign commands to function keys using the Function Keys dialog box, pictured in Figure 12.2.

The left column is where you key in the function key's name, which will appear in a button at the bottom of the screen. The right column is where you key in the command that you wish the function key to execute. The Key Level option buttons allow you to switch to a new set of eight function key assignments.

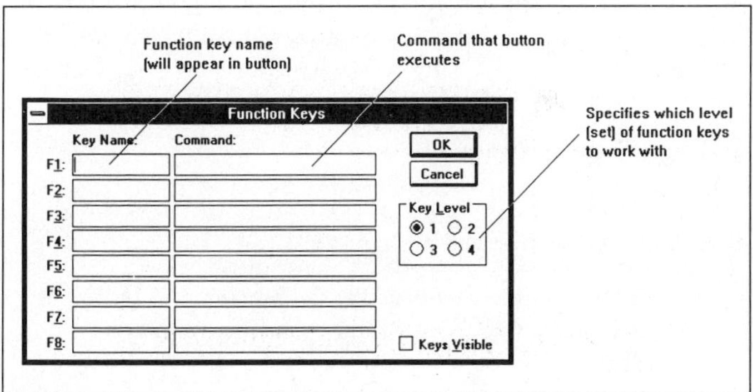

Figure 12.2: The Function Keys dialog box

To Use the Mouse

1. Pull down the Settings menu and select Function Keys. The dialog box in Figure 12.2 will appear.
2. Type the desired name for the F1 function key button in the Key Name text box.
3. Click on the adjacent Command text box, then type the command you wish the function key to execute.
4. Repeat steps 2 and 3 for each function key, if desired.
5. Click on a Key Level option button, if desired, to make a new set of commands available, then repeat steps 2 and 3.
6. Click on OK.

INVOKING A FUNCTION KEY

• **EXPLANATION** Invoking a function key means that you click on or press a function key button and that the command associated with that key or button is executed.

To Use the Mouse

The function key buttons must first be visible (see "Displaying the Function Keys" earlier in this chapter).

- Place the mouse pointer over the function key button at the bottom of the screen, and click. The command assigned to that button will execute.

To Use the Keyboard

1. Press and hold down the Ctrl and Alt keys, then press the function key that executes the command you want.
2. After the command executes, release the Ctrl and Alt keys.

CHANGING COMMUNICATIONS PARAMETERS

• EXPLANATION Terminal's communications parameters are the settings that determine how the program communicates with the serial port and modem. They are:

- Baud Rate—a measurement of the speed at which serial transmission takes place. It specifies the number of times per second that the serial port changes the electric signals it is transmitting from +5 volts or more to –5 volts or less.
- Data Bits—specifies the number of bits that comprise a word. A bit is a binary digit, either one or zero; it is the unit of information that the serial port transmits. A word is a group of bits used to denote characters and other forms of data. A word can be five, six, seven, or eight bits long.
- Stop Bits—a group of bits that signify the end of a data transmission packet. There can be either one, one and a half, or two stop bits.
- Parity—an error correction scheme used by the serial port. There are five types of parity: even, odd, none, mark, and space. Most systems expect you to use none.
- Flow Control—sets the method, or protocol, by which the flow of data is controlled. This setting applies only to terminal emulation and the transmission of textual data; the flow control protocol used for binary file transfers will probably be different.
- Connector (serial port)—specifies DOS's name for the serial port you want Terminal to use. DOS serial ports are named COM1, COM2, COM3, and COM4.
- Carrier Detect—instructs Terminal to use the carrier detect signal line on the RS-232 port to determine if the telephone signal is lost. Check this box when you want Terminal to hang up automatically when the telephone

signal is lost. This works with Hayes-compatible modems, and may or may not work with other modems.

All of these settings are controlled via option buttons and check boxes in the Communications dialog box.

To Use the Mouse

1. Pull down the Settings menu and select Communications. The Communications dialog box will appear.
2. Set the desired communications parameter.
3. Click on OK.

CHANGING TERMINAL EMULATION

• **EXPLANATION** Terminal communicates with larger computer systems by emulating a standard terminal. Terminal emulates three types of terminals: a teletype machine (TTY), the DEC VT-100 (the default emulation), and the DEC VT-52. The VT-100 emulation will also accept standard ANSI control sequences, which are used by most public bulletin boards to draw menus and simple graphics on terminal screens.

To Use the Mouse

1. Pull down the Settings menu and select Terminal Emulation. The Terminal Emulation dialog box will appear.
2. Click on the option button for the desired terminal emulation, then click on OK.

CHANGING TERMINAL SETTINGS

• EXPLANATION The terminal emulation that Terminal uses can be configured in many ways. For example, you can use 80 or 132 columns, and you can specify the font to use in the emulation. The specific settings you can control are:

- Line Wrap—specifies whether or not Terminal will automatically display incoming text on the next line, when that text exceeds the specified column setting. The default setting for Line Wrap is on.
- Local Echo—tells Terminal to echo (display) on screen any character typed at the keyboard. The default setting is for no local echo.
- Sound—tells Terminal to sound a beep whenever it receives a bell character (Ctrl-G). By default, Terminal will beep.
- Carriage Return/Line Feed—tells Terminal how to interpret carriage returns. With the Inbound check box selected, Terminal will add a line feed to any inbound carriage return. With the Outbound check box selected, Terminal will add a line feed to any outbound carriage return. By default, Terminal adds no line feeds to carriage returns.
- Cursor (size)—sets the cursor to a block, an underline, a blinking block, or a blinking underline. The default setting is a blinking block.
- Columns—specifies whether the screen should have 80 or 132 columns. The default is 80.
- Terminal Font—determines the type of font and the point size used to display text. The default is usually the System font at 15 points.

- Translation—sets the desired international character set for translation of textual data. Terminal uses as the default whatever character set you specified when you installed Windows.
- Show Scroll Bars—specifies whether or not scroll bars appear on the Terminal window. By default, they do appear.
- Buffer Lines—sets the desired number of lines for the scroll buffer (the number of previously displayed lines that you can scroll back through). The default is 100.

All of these settings are accessed using the Terminal Preferences dialog box.

To Use the Mouse

1. Pull down the Settings menu and select Terminal Preferences. The Terminal Preferences dialog box will appear.
2. Change the desired terminal setting.
3. Click on OK.

CAPTURING A TEXT FILE

• **EXPLANATION** Terminal has the ability to capture every character that appears on the Terminal screen and save it to an ASCII text file. You should perform the procedure described below just before the text you want to capture appears on screen.

To Use the Mouse

1. Pull down the Transfers menu and select Receive Text File. The Receive Text File dialog box will appear.
2. Type the name of the new file in which you wish to store the received text, or click on the name of an existing file. When you specify the name of an existing file, Terminal overwrites it. If you click on the Append File check box,

Terminal will not overwrite the file, but instead append the new text to the text that already exists.

3. Click on OK. Terminal will display the number of bytes received in the status line at the bottom of the screen.
4. When you have captured all the text you want, pull down the Transfers menu and select Stop. Terminal will close the file.

SETTING A BINARY TRANSFER PROTOCOL

• **EXPLANATION** A binary transfer protocol is a set of rules for software to follow when transferring files between two computers. The software on both the sending and receiving computers must be using the same protocol. Terminal uses two protocols: XMODEM/CRC and Kermit.

To Use the Mouse

1. Pull down the Settings menu and select Binary Transfers. The Binary Transfers dialog box will appear.
2. Click on the option button for the desired protocol.
3. Click on OK.

UPLOADING A BINARY FILE

• **EXPLANATION** To upload a binary file is to send a file from your computer to another computer. Before you can send a file, you must first make sure that both Terminal and the receiving computer are using the same transfer protocol. (See "Setting a Binary Transfer Protocol," above.)

To Use the Mouse

1. Instruct the computer you are communicating with (called the host system) to receive a file. The procedure for doing this differs between host systems.
2. Pull down the Transfers menu and select Send Binary File. The Send Binary File dialog box will appear.
3. Key in the name of the file you wish to send, or select the file from the Files list box.
4. Click on OK. The file transfer will begin. Terminal will display a scale showing the progress of the transfer.

DOWNLOADING A BINARY FILE

• **EXPLANATION** To download a binary file is to have another computer send a file to your computer. Before you can receive a file, you must first make sure that both Terminal and the sending computer are using the same transfer protocol. (See "Setting a Binary Transfer Protocol" in this chapter.)

To Use the Mouse

1. Instruct the computer you are communicating with (called the host system) to send a file. The procedure for doing this differs between host systems.
2. Pull down the Transfers menu and select Receive Binary File. A dialog box will appear, asking you to specify a name for the file.
3. Type a name for the file.

4. Click on OK. The file transfer will begin. Terminal will display a status line at the bottom of the screen that will indicate how many bytes have been received and how many errors and retrys have occurred.

Chapter 13

MISCELLANEOUS ACCESSORY PROGRAMS

CARDFILE

Windows Cardfile is a limited-use flat-file database program that imitates a desktop Rolodex. It lets you create "index cards" on screen, sort them, view them, and use them to automatically dial a telephone number printed on the card. Cardfile is designed to replace the standard business Rolodex file found on many desks.

The standard Cardfile screen is composed of four parts; see Figure 13.1. These parts consist of:

- The status line—this line tells you what type of view is in effect and how many cards are in the current card file.
- The index line—this line holds text, and is the sort key for the entire card file. You can type anything you want here, but if you are using Cardfile as a Rolodex, it's probably wise to type a last name and a first name here.
- The scroll arrows—the left arrow moves you through the cards backward and the right arrow moves you through the cards forward.
- The information area—this rectangular area is where you type the information you want on the card.

RUNNING CARDFILE

• EXPLANATION Cardfile is a Windows application whose icon is in the Accessories program group.

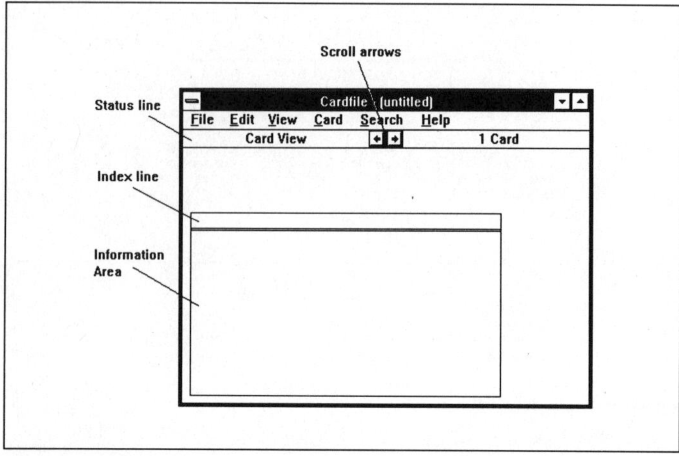

Figure 13.1: A standard Cardfile screen

To Use the Mouse

1. Open the Accessories program group.
2. Double-click on the Cardfile icon, which is a picture of a desktop Rolodex file. The Cardfile window will appear with a blank card displayed in its workspace.

CREATING/EDITING A CARD

• EXPLANATION When Cardfile first runs, there is a blank card visible in its workspace.

To Use the Mouse

1. Double-click on the card's index line. A dialog box prompting you to key in the index text will appear.
2. Type the index text (usually a last name and a first name), then click on OK. The Cardfile window will reappear. There will be a blinking vertical cursor in the upper-left corner of the information area.

3. Type the information you want on the card. You may want to follow the standard convention for typing a name and address here, with one exception. Make sure you type the phone number *before* the zip code or any other number. That's because when Cardfile autodials, it searches the information area for the first number it finds and then uses it as the telephone number.

ADDING A CARD

• EXPLANATION As you use Cardfile, you will probably need to add new cards to your file.

To Use the Mouse

1. Pull down the Card menu and select Add. The Add dialog box will appear. Though there is no indication of it, this is where you key in the index line for the new card.
2. Type the index text (usually a last name and a first name), then click on OK. The Cardfile window will reappear with the new card at the forefront. There will be a blinking vertical cursor in the upper-left corner of the information area.
3. Type the information you want on the card.

See Also Creating/Editing a Card

SAVING A CARD FILE

• EXPLANATION Cardfile saves cards in a disk file so you can use the cards at a later time. The files are saved in a format only Cardfile can read. They are stored in the Windows directory unless you specify otherwise.

To Use the Mouse

1. Pull down the File menu and select Save. If the card file has been previously saved, this step is the only one you need to take. If the file has not been saved previously, a

dialog box will appear, prompting you for the name of the card file.

2. Type the desired name, leaving off the file extension. Cardfile will automatically add a .CRD extension.
3. Click on OK.

OPENING A CARD FILE

• **EXPLANATION** Before Cardfile can work with previously created card files, they must be loaded into Cardfile from disk.

To Use the Mouse

1. Pull down the File menu and select Open. A dialog box listing the available card files will appear.
2. Type the name of the card file to load, or click on its name in the list box.
3. Click on OK. Cardfile will read the card file from disk.

DELETING A CARD

• **EXPLANATION** A card file can become crowded with outdated names and addresses; you will sometimes need to delete a card.

To Use the Mouse

1. Bring the card you wish to delete to the front of the stack by clicking in its index line.
2. Pull down the Card menu and select Delete. A dialog box will appear, asking you to confirm the deletion.
3. Click on OK. The card will be deleted.

CHANGING THE CARD VIEW

• **EXPLANATION** Cardfile offers two ways for you to view a card file: the Card view and the List view. In the Card view, you are looking at a stack of index cards, with one card visible on the top of the stack and the index lines of the other cards visible. In the List view, the index lines of the cards are presented in list format, and the information on the cards is not visible. The List view comes in handy when you have a great many cards and you need to look through them quickly.

To Use the Mouse

1. Pull down the View menu and select List. The Cardfile workspace will change to a list of the index lines on all the cards.
2. Click on the index line of the card you wish to see.
3. Pull down the View menu and select Card. Cardfile will switch back to the Card view, and the selected card will be at the top of the stack.

MERGING CARD FILES

• **EXPLANATION** Cardfile lets you merge multiple card files into a single file.

To Use the Mouse

1. Open one of the files to be merged.
2. Pull down the File menu and select Merge. A dialog box will appear with a list of the available card files in it.
3. Type the name of the card file you wish to merge into the open file, or click on the file's name in the list box.
4. Click on OK.

USING AUTODIAL

• **EXPLANATION** If your computer is attached to a standard Hayes or Hayes-compatible modem, Cardfile can use the telephone number listed in the information area to dial your telephone.

The autodial feature of Cardfile scans all the text in a card and uses the first number it finds as the telephone number. So make sure when you type information on a card that the first number that appears is the phone number.

To Use the Mouse

Start by making sure that the card containing the number you wish to dial is at the top of the card stack.

1. Pull down the Card menu and select Autodial. The Autodial dialog box will appear.
2. If you have autodialed previously, go to step 4. If you are autodialing for the first time, click on the Setup command button. The Autodial dialog box will expand and display option buttons for telling Cardfile the baud rate of the modem, the type of dialing the phone uses, and the serial port in use.
3. Configure each of these settings to match your system.
4. Click on OK.

Notes The Autodial feature supports system-specific prefixes, such as dialing 9 from an office to get an outside line (to do this, type the desired prefix and toggle the Use Prefix option on). However, it has no way of knowing if it is dialing a long-distance or local number. If your area requires you to dial 1 before dialing a long-distance number, make sure that numeral is part of those numbers. A local number on a card might read "555-1234," while a long-distance number would read "1 404 555-1234."

FINDING TEXT

• EXPLANATION Cardfile will search all the cards in a card file for any text you specify. Cardfile will search for the text only on the cards themselves, not on the index lines, and will not differentiate between whole words and parts of words.

To Use the Mouse

1. Pull down the Search menu and select Find. A dialog box will appear, asking you to key in the text for which you wish to search.
2. Type the text you wish to search for, then click on OK. Cardfile will find the first occurrence of the specified text. To continue searching through the file for the same text, pull down the Search menu and select Find Next.

PRINTING A CARD FILE

• **EXPLANATION** Printing a card file is much like printing from any other Windows program. You can either print a single card, or print all the cards in a file.

To Use the Mouse

1. If you are printing a single card, place the card you wish to print at the front of the file by clicking on its index line.
2. Pull down the File menu and select Print if you are printing a single card, Print All if you are printing all of the cards.

CALENDAR

Windows Calendar is a combination monthly calendar and daily appointment book program. You can use Calendar to keep track of appointments, vacations, paydays, holidays, and more.

Calendar displays time in two ways: as a monthly calendar, called the Month view, and as a list of daily appointments, called the Day view. The Day view display is pictured in Figure 13.2.

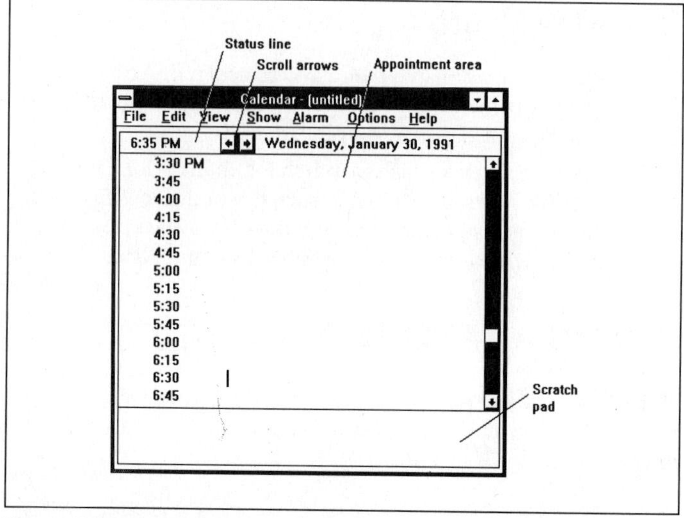

Figure 13.2: The Day view screen

The scroll arrows in the Day view increment the appointment list by one day; when the Month view is displayed, they increment the calendar by one month.

RUNNING CALENDAR

• **EXPLANATION** Calendar is a Windows application whose icon is in the Accessories program group.

To Use the Mouse

1. Open the Accessories program group.
2. Double-click on the Calendar icon, which is an image of a desktop calendar. The Calendar window will appear, with the daily appointment list displayed in its workspace.

ENTERING AN APPOINTMENT

• **EXPLANATION** Calendar allows you to enter an appointment in the displayed appointment list at any time. (To control how time is displayed—by hour, quarter-hour, half-hour—see "Changing Hour/Minute Display" later in this chapter.)

To Use the Mouse

Start from the Day (appointment list) view.

1. Move the mouse pointer into the appointment area, directly to the right of the appointment time, and click. A blinking, upright cursor will appear adjacent to the time.
2. Type text describing the appointment.
3. Press ↵ to move to the next available appointment time, or click the mouse as in step 1.

SETTING AN ALARM

• **EXPLANATION** Calendar will set an alarm to inform you of an appointment. If Calendar is active and on screen, the alarm will take the form of a dialog box. If Calendar is inactive and on screen, its title bar will flash. If Calendar is an icon, the icon will flash. In all cases, a beep will sound when the alarm goes off.

To Use the Mouse

Start from the Day (appointment list) view.

1. Move the mouse pointer over the appointment for which you wish to set an alarm, and click. A vertical, blinking cursor will appear in the appointment text.
2. Pull down the Alarm menu and click on Set. A figure of a bell will appear beside the specified time to indicate that the alarm has been set.

See Also Setting Early Alarm Ring and Sound

SETTING EARLY ALARM RING AND SOUND

• EXPLANATION Once an alarm has been set, you have the option of customizing it so that it rings up to ten minutes before the appointment, allowing you time to prepare. You can also specify that no beep sounds when the alarm goes off, which means that you will have only a visual indication of the alarm.

To Use the Mouse

1. Set an alarm. (See "Setting an Alarm" earlier in this chapter.)
2. Pull down the Alarm menu and select Controls. A dialog box will appear with a text box and a check box inside it.
3. Key a number between 1 and 10 into the Early Ring text box. This will be the number of minutes before the appointment that the alarm will ring.
4. If you like, clear the Sound check box by clicking on it, and the alarm will make no sound.
5. Click on OK.

CHANGING THE VIEW

• EXPLANATION Calendar displays time in two ways, as a monthly calendar and as a list of daily appointments. Toggling between the two is described below. You can also toggle quickly between the daily and monthly views by double-clicking on the date in the status line.

To Use the Mouse

Starting from the Day (appointment list) view:

1. Pull down the View menu and click on Month. The display will change to a monthly calendar.

2. To toggle back to the Day view, pull down the View menu and click on Day.

To Use the Keyboard

- Press F9 to Switch to the Month view. Press F8 to switch to the Day view.

CHANGING HOUR/MINUTE DISPLAY

• EXPLANATION Calendar lets you change the time scale displayed in the Day view. You can make and display appointments for times on the hour, half-hour, or quarter-hour. You can also specify the starting time for each daily appointment list, and change the display from the 12-hour day to the 24-hour day used by the military.

To Use the Mouse

1. Pull down the Options menu and select Day Settings. A dialog box will appear with two sets of option buttons and a text box in it.
2. Set the interval at which you want times displayed by clicking on one of the Interval option buttons.
3. Change the hour format by clicking on one of the Hour Format option buttons.
4. To change the starting time for the daily appointment list, click on the Starting Time text box, then key in the time. Make sure to use a colon to separate the hours and minutes.
5. Click on OK.

ADDING OR DELETING A SPECIAL TIME

• EXPLANATION A special time is a time that is not usually displayed in the Day view because it does not fall on the hour, half-hour, or quarter-hour. If you have an appointment at a special time, Calendar will insert the time in the Day view, allowing you to list the appointment. Special times can be inserted only on individual days; you can't automatically make a special time appear on all days.

To Add a Special Time Using the Mouse

1. Pull down the Options menu and select Special Time. A dialog box will appear.
2. Type the special time in the Special Time text box. Be sure to separate the hours and minutes with a colon.
3. Click on the Insert command button. The special time will appear in the appointment list.

To Delete a Special Time Using the Mouse

1. In the Day view appointment list, click on the special time you wish to delete.
2. Pull down the Options menu and select Special Time. A dialog box will appear with the special time displayed in the text box.
3. Click on the Delete command button. The special time will be deleted from the appointment list.

SHOWING DAYS AND MONTHS

• EXPLANATION Calendar can show you the next or previous daily schedule or monthly calendar in sequence, depending on whether it is using Day or Month view. Calendar will also display the schedule or calendar for any day you specify, as long as the date is between January 1, 1980 and December 31, 2099.

To Show a Sequential Day or Month

Mouse

- Pull down the Show menu and select Previous or Next, depending on which schedule or calendar you want to view.

Keyboard

- To move to the previous schedule or calendar, press Ctrl-PgUp. To move to the next schedule or calendar, press Ctrl-PgDn.

To Show a Specific Day

Mouse

1. Pull down the Show menu and select Date. A dialog box will appear, asking you to key in the date you wish to show.
2. Type in the date using one of three formats: dd/mm/yy, dd-mm-yy, or dd/mm/yyyy.
3. Click on OK.

Keyboard

1. Press F4. A dialog box will appear, asking you to key in the date you wish to show.
2. Type in the date using one of three formats: dd/mm/yy, dd-mm-yy, or dd/mm/yyyy. If you have installed Windows to use a different date format, you must key in the data according to that format. In any format, you can truncate the year to the last two digits and Windows will assume you mean the twentieth century, not the twenty-first (1990, for example, not 2090).
3. Press ↵.

MARKING A DAY

• EXPLANATION When you use Calendar in the Month view, you can mark individual days with one of five symbols. By assigning a symbol to a specific type of day, such as a holiday, you can easily tell when in the month that day occurs.

To Use the Mouse

Start with Calendar in the Month view.

1. Select the day you wish to mark.
2. Pull down the Options menu and select Mark. The Day Markings dialog box will appear. It will have four check boxes in it, for four symbols: square brackets, parentheses, a lowercase "o," a lowercase "x," and an underline.
3. Select the symbol with which you want to mark the day. You can select more than one symbol.
4. Click on OK.

CALCULATOR

One of the accessory programs shipped with Windows is Calculator. Calculator imitates both standard (algebraic) and scientific hand-held calculators.

In Standard mode, Calculator performs addition, subtraction, multiplication, and division; it derives square roots, percentages, and reciprocals; it also has memory storage and recall features. In Scientific mode, Calculator performs hexadecimal, decimal, octal, and binary math; it also has statistical, logarithmic, exponential, and logical functions.

RUNNING CALCULATOR

• **EXPLANATION** Calculator is a Windows application whose icon is in the Accessories program group.

To Use the Mouse

1. Open the Accessories program group.
2. Double-click on the Calculator icon, which is a picture of a hand-held calculator. The Calculator window appears, in whatever mode it was last in. The default mode is Standard.

CHANGING TO THE SCIENTIFIC CALCULATOR

• **EXPLANATION** The scientific calculator is useful for people doing programming, statistical mathematics, or advanced algebra.

To Use the Mouse

1. Pull down the View menu and select Scientific. The scientific calculator will appear.
2. To switch back to the standard calculator, pull down the View menu and select Standard.

CLOCK

Another accessory program included with Windows is Clock, which provides an onscreen clock. When minimized to an icon, Clock continues to keep the correct time and displays it in the icon. Since Clock only uses about 12K of memory, you can keep a timepiece on your Windows desktop just as you would on your real desktop.

RUNNING CLOCK

• **EXPLANATION** Clock is a Windows application whose icon is in the Accessories program group.

To Use the Mouse

1. Open the Accessories program group.
2. Double-click on the Clock icon, which is a picture of a clock. The Clock window appears in whatever mode it was last in. The default mode is Analog.

CHANGING TO ANALOG OR DIGITAL CLOCK

• EXPLANATION Clock displays time in two formats: analog and digital. An analog clock is circular and has hour, minute, and sweep second hands. A digital clock displays the current time in hours, minutes, and seconds in the format HH:MM:SS.

To Use the Mouse

- Pull down the Settings menu and select Analog or Digital.

Index

U

V

W

X

Z

SYBEX Computer Books are different.

Here is why . . .

At SYBEX, each book is designed with you in mind. Every manuscript is carefully selected and supervised by our editors, who are themselves computer experts. We publish the best authors, whose technical expertise is matched by an ability to write clearly and to communicate effectively. Programs are thoroughly tested for accuracy by our technical staff. Our computerized production department goes to great lengths to make sure that each book is well-designed.

In the pursuit of timeliness, SYBEX has achieved many publishing firsts. SYBEX was among the first to integrate personal computers used by authors and staff into the publishing process. SYBEX was the first to publish books on the CP/M operating system, microprocessor interfacing techniques, word processing, and many more topics.

Expertise in computers and dedication to the highest quality product have made SYBEX a world leader in computer book publishing. Translated into fourteen languages, SYBEX books have helped millions of people around the world to get the most from their computers. We hope we have helped you, too.

Windows Shortcut Keys

In Write

KEY SEQUENCE	EFFECT
F3	Find next occurrence
F4	Jump to specific page
F5	Make text normal
Ctrl-B	Make text boldfaced
Ctrl-I	Make text italic
Ctrl-U	Make text underlined
Ctrl-↵	Insert page break

In Paintbrush

KEY SEQUENCE	EFFECT
Ctrl-Z	Zoom in
Ctrl-O	Zoom out
Ctrl-C	View picture
Ctrl-B	Make text boldfaced
Ctrl-I	Make text italic
Ctrl-U	Make text underlined
Ins	Left mouse button click
Del	Right mouse button click
F9-Ins	Left mouse button double-click
F9-Del	Right mouse button double-click